ADULTING MADE SIMPLE - FROM BASICS TO BEYOND

Life Skills for Older Teens and Adults. Flex Your Confidence, Unlock Money Hacks, And Master the Secret Art of Surviving and Thriving in the Real World

---

K.A. BROOKS

Table of Contents

Introduction

Do you ever look back and think about when you were younger, and everything seemed simpler? No worries about how the heck you will be able to pay for bills, how to stretch your income to make ends meet, how to create a good first impression at job interviews, or how to get prepared for retirement days; just the freedom to explore the world and enjoy the life that your parents have provided for you. After all, your biggest concerns might be whether you can finish your homework on time or figure out things to do over the weekend. But as we grow older, we start to see a different side of life, which is often harsher than we've probably thought. We begin to relate to our older brother, sister, or even parents, who sometimes seem stressed about bills to pay and handling serious issues that come their way out of nowhere. It's that horrifying moment when you're looking for an adult and realize you are an adult.

Let's face it, adulting indeed sucks, especially for you who are fresh out of the warmth and comfort of your parent's house. If you ever think about how exciting it is to no longer have a curfew, be able to eat whatever you want, stay up late as you want, and do whatever your heart desires, how do you feel right now, at the edge of adulthood? Does it still feel thrilling? Being an adult seemed pretty great until you realized... that it wasn't. It truly feels like being handed the keys to a car without knowing how to drive—or even which side the gas goes in.

In your journey toward adulthood, you'll often be left wondering why topics like how to land a job, how to budget, how to start investing, how to take care of yourself, and how to comply with legal responsibilities were never part of your education. Instead, you were often pushed to memorize the sequence of photosynthesis, Pythagoras' theorem, and all those historical dates and events that have nothing to do with the reality awaiting you. Yeah, that gap between what school teaches and what life throws at you can feel wider than the Grand Canyon. Well, it is a frustrating reality, leaving you constantly wondering, "Why wasn't I prepared for this?"

That's where I come in. I've been right where you are, standing on the edge of adulthood, wondering if I could build a raft out of my diplomas to float back to the simplicity of school days. But I learned to navigate these waters, and now, my passion and purpose are to pass on that map to you. My experiences, combined with a genuine desire to make adulting less of a chore, have inspired me to create this guide. After all, I don't want you to make the same mistakes I did and be left feeling alone. While I can't prevent you from making mistakes (because, let's face it, they're sometimes inevitable), through this book, I can help you prepare for the road ahead by minimizing common detours caused by manageable and preventable mistakes.

Adulting Made Simple: From Basics to Beyond isn't your average guide to adulting. Think of it as your personalized, choose-your-own-adventure book for navigating the complexities of modern life. This book is for all the older teens and adults who want to "make it," "have it all," and, most importantly, feel confident in tackling what life throws at them but aren't sure where to start. I'm talking about financial literacy, understanding your digital footprint, managing your mental and physical health, mastering practical life skills, and building relationships that don't just exist on social media.

To my fellow older teens and adults: I see you. I know the mix of excitement and anxiety that comes with this new chapter. I understand that navigating adulthood in this era can be particularly challenging, whether dealing with economic insecurity, uncertainty, isolation, or even an itch to stay updated. The list goes on, leaving you constantly comparing yourself to those unrealistic public figures, which often triggers feelings of not doing enough. But the truth is, we're all struggling in our own ways to figure things out. That's why this book is crafted with you in mind, addressing not only the timeless challenges of transitioning into adulthood but also the unique hurdles of our digital era.

However, this book is more than just old time-worn advice passed down from generation to generation without any tweaks. It's a well-blended mix of current research, expert advice, and practical steps, all woven together with engaging stories and real-life examples. It's designed for you to dive in wherever it feels most relevant. Want to tackle managing your finances head-on? Go for it. Curious about mental health? There's a chapter for that, too. With this book, the goal is for you to confidently tackle whatever comes your way.

As you turn these pages, I encourage you not just to read but to engage. Reflect on the exercises, jot down notes, and apply what you learn. With a bit of determination and this book in hand, I'm confident you can navigate the challenges of adulting. Let this book banish your self-doubt about "How come nobody ever told me that adulthood is hard?" and replace it with, "Well, adulthood does get easier as I grow better at it."

Before we embark on this adventure together, I want to leave you with a personal note. I sincerely hope this book helps you on your path to independence. Remember, you are not alone in this journey. Together, we'll laugh, maybe cry a bit, but most importantly, we'll grow. So, buckle up, and let's make adulting a little less daunting and a lot more doable. Welcome to your guide to thriving in the real world.

ONE

Academic and Career Development

J ust seconds ago, you were thrilled about your high school graduation, marking the complete transition from adolescence to adulthood, which at the same time symbolizes newfound independence. While some of your friends already have their plans laid out ahead of them, you, like many others, may be experiencing a mix of feelings: fear and uncertainty, especially when deciding on the next steps in academic and career development.

You may just be realizing now that along with the no curfews, rigid school schedules, or constant parental supervision that you've always wanted comes the need to make your own choices and chart your own course. The feeling that your future is wide open in your hands can be both exhilarating and intimidating. Choosing a college, career, or even just figuring out "what to do next" can easily become overwhelming as you have countless options and conflicting advice swirling in your mind.

At the same time, you need to deal with the pressure to make the "right" decision and deal with the many "what ifs" surrounding your head right now: What if I choose the wrong path? What if I miss out on something better? The fear goes on.

The fear and uncertainty surrounding adulthood can feel endless; however, you are not alone. Everyone—literally everyone—battles with their own thoughts daily on whether they've made the right decision or not, even into their 20s or 30s. Nothing will be perfect. So, rather than dwelling on your thoughts, which at times often only result in negativity, use this transition time to explore different paths, interests, and experiences that will facilitate you in choosing a path that allows you to acquire valuable skills and knowledge, even if you're still unsure of the exact destination. Celebrate this journey as a time of growth and discovery.

Educational Pathways: Choosing a College or Trade School

Ah, the classic spiel about four-year college being the promised land, the Holy Grail, and the only option everyone seems to shove down your throat, right? Sure, it's the go-to recommendation from almost everyone, including your parents and most teachers. But let's not forget there's a whole array of educational options out there that might just tickle your fancy more, each offering different opportunities for further learning and skill development. Just as you wouldn't want to wear the same outfits as everyone else, why should you feel pressured to choose your post-high school path based on what others think you should do? So, buckle up! Below are some common education programs you should consider before deciding which one to dive into.

- **Colleges:** A traditional four-year college offers bachelor's degree programs across a wide range of fields, from arts and humanities to business, education, engineering, health and sciences, social sciences, and more. Colleges provide their students with a broad foundation, better preparing them for diverse careers or further academic pursuits, such as master's or even doctoral programs. Plus, college students have many opportunities for extracurricular activities, networking, and gaining leadership experience. Thus, those who are committed to pursuing a bachelor's degree, value academic rigor and intellectual exploration, and seek a comprehensive college experience through clubs and organizations may be suitable for attending college. However, as college can be costly, you'll need to make sure you already know what field you want to study. Aside from the conventional classroom-based college experience, you can also opt for online college courses, which provide more flexibility, especially if balancing them with work commitments. Many reputable colleges offer online degree programs and courses, allowing you to earn associate's, bachelor's, or even master's degrees entirely online. However, ensure that your chosen online institution is accredited and suitable for your academic goals. Other than traditional four-year colleges, you can pursue associate degrees, typically completed in two years of full-time study. These degrees can prepare you for specific careers or serve as stepping stones before transferring to a four-year college. Or, if you're interested in completing certificate programs or workforce training alongside your associate degree, a community college might be the right choice. Compared to four-year institutions, community colleges are often more affordable, making them suitable for those looking to save money or explore different career paths before committing to longer academic programs.

- **Trade schools:** Trade schools, also known as technical schools, offer specialized training and education in specific crafts or trades, ranging from automotive technology, culinary arts, cosmetology, plumbing, welding, electrical work, and more. Not all professions require a formal degree, so attending trade schools can provide you with skills and specific knowledge tailored to your chosen field. Compared to colleges, programs at trade schools are typically shorter, lasting as little as a few months to two years; upon completion, students can earn a certificate. The program focuses on practical instruction and knowledge necessary to prepare students for entry-level positions in their chosen fields. Hence, they typically spend most of their time in workshops, labs, and simulated work environments, gaining firsthand real-world experience under experienced instructors' close guidance. In terms of cost, trade school programs are often more affordable than four-year college programs due to their shorter duration and less emphasis on general education courses. Therefore, attending trade school is an attractive option for those who prefer to start earning income quickly, especially if they know precisely what they want to pursue professionally after high school.

- **Apprenticeship programs:** Similar to trade schools, apprenticeship programs provide a blend of practical experience and theoretical knowledge necessary under the supervision of professionals. However, apprenticeship programs also offer paid on-the-job training, allowing you to earn a salary while learning. In some cases, students attending these programs may be able to cover the cost of tuition, materials, and training-related expenses. Regarding cost, duration, and certification upon completion, apprenticeship programs are similar to trade schools, although they may vary depending on the chosen program. Additionally, certain apprenticeship programs may require specific qualifications or pre-apprenticeship training. Therefore, if you know the particular field you want to pursue professionally and are highly committed to working hard both in the classroom and on the job while getting paid, apprenticeship programs can be the right fit for you. Plus, these programs can lead to continued employment within the company depending on the company's needs and your own performance.

After having all the options laid out, what makes you start choosing one among the others? Many people may say follow your passion and interest. Well, it is undoubtedly important to follow your passion, but let's be real: It is equally important to consider the realities of the job market and earning potential. Of course, nobody wants to struggle to make ends meet. Also, even if you're passionate about a specific field, you need to ensure your chosen field has enough job opportunities and career growth potential to sustain you in the long run. However, it is not about sacrificing your dreams but finding the sweet spot where your heart's desires meet the working world's practicalities.

To start balancing those out, let yourself explore a wide range of fields that align with your passion and interest while keeping an open mind to non-traditional job options. Then, assess job market trends within the last few years and earning potential in your chosen fields. It is not about projecting to the highest income job, but most importantly, considering the long-term growth potential.

Financial Aid and Scholarships: You Know Where You Want to Go, Now What?

So, you've got your mind set on diving into a specific educational program, you've figured out what you want to study, and you're itching to get started. But then, the big question hits: How on earth am I going to pay for it? It often feels like walking a tightrope between wanting the best education possible and not wanting to burden your parents with more bills to pay. Growing up, we've all seen the sweat and sacrifices our parents put in to provide for the family. It's only natural if we don't want to add to their plate with our hefty education costs. Trust me, you are not alone. Pretty much everyone your age has been through the same thing. After all, by taking control of your education funding, you're taking charge of yourself and charting your own course. That's where stuff like scholarships, financial aid, and figuring out how to manage the costs come into play, each having different ways to help foot the bill for your education.

When it comes to educational funding, scholarships might be the first thing that comes to mind. Scholarships are typically awarded based on your grades, talents, leadership skills, community involvement, or background to help you pursue education. Getting a scholarship means getting money you don't have to pay back for tuition fees and, in some cases, educational expenses, which is a huge win! Not limited to colleges and universities, scholarships can also be provided by government agencies, private organizations, corporations, or foundations.

However, finding scholarship opportunities that match your profile can be a bit like searching for hidden treasure. So, don't wait till those opportunities come your way at the last minute; start exploring them as soon as possible, even when you are still in your junior year of high school. Besides scouring online scholarship platforms, try to match your unique qualities and interests with the scholarships out there. Furthermore, exploring scholarship opportunities early means more time to prepare a strong application. So, once you've shortlisted a few scholarships you want to apply for, it's time to craft compelling applications. It begins with paying close attention to each scholarship's requirements and instructions to avoid getting the boot before you even start. Then, be sure to highlight all your academic achievements, extracurricular activities, leadership roles, and community service, especially those that best match the scholarship criteria. As many scholarships require you to submit a personal essay, use this opportunity to express your aspirations and show why you deserve the scholarship. However, remember to be honest, be passionate, and get a second opinion from someone you trust before hitting send.

In addition to scholarships, there are various options for financial assistance, including grants, loans, and work-study opportunities, which should be taken into account. Similar to scholarships, grants have no repayment requirements. They are given out in accordance with the provider's specified criteria, financial need, or academic performance—whether it's the government, organizations, or universities. Although the qualifying requirements for each grant may differ, it is often necessary to prove financial need by completing FAFSA, an application for federal student aid. On the other hand, loans provide educational funding that must be repaid with interest according to the terms and conditions set by the lender. Federal loans typically offer more favorable terms and conditions than private loans. Meanwhile, work-study programs that provide part-time employment possibilities are worth considering if you're interested in earning money while studying. To determine if you qualify for this program, you must also complete the FAFSA.

Since most financial aid programs, primarily federal, state, and institutional-based ones, require the FAFSA to determine eligibility, you should be familiar with it. The FAFSA collects details about your family's income, assets, household size, and other factors to assess financial need. Every year, if you want to be considered for federal student aid, you must complete a new FAFSA form. The application typically opens on October 1st each year, so submit it as early as possible for better consideration. To help fill out the FAFSA, plan on contacting your school counselor.

So, you've sorted your financial aid—whether it's a scholarship, grant, loan, or work-study program. Great job! But now comes the part where you've got to be smart about managing your expenses to make sure you don't drown in debt while pursuing your education. First things first, you've got to allocate every dollar wisely—tuition, books, living costs —they all add up. When you decide to take out loans, you must borrow only what you absolutely need, even though I know it's tempting to borrow extra for those spur-of-the-moment splurges. Remember, every dollar you borrow today must be repaid later—and worse—with interest. So, always try to live within or even below your means.

When it comes to cutting costs, try to think outside of the box. Are your textbooks expensive? Look for used books at bookstores or online platforms. Is renting near college burning a hole in your wallet? Explore cheaper housing options like dorms or shared apartments. Do you need some extra cash? Channel your inner entrepreneur and sell your creations or services online. Don't worry; there's a market for almost anything. And hey, get your priorities straight. Do you really need the latest smartphone or that fancy coffee every day? Do you really need to eat out instead of cooking meals at home? Get creative and resourceful—you'll be surprised at how much you can save by thinking outside the box.

Student Loans Demystified: Strategies for Management and Repayment

Ah, the joy of scholarships and grants—it's like hitting the jackpot, right? Well, for most of us, it's more like playing the lottery and never even getting a free ticket. That's why so many people, or maybe you're one of them, end up taking loans. Sure, it's a bit of a bummer not to be one of the chosen few blessed with free educational cash, especially when you've been sweating bullets trying to snag them. But fear not! You are not alone—well, it's actually super common. In fact, over 92 million Americans have experienced the burden of student loan debt at some point in their lives (Hanson, 2022). It's not as ideal as getting grants and scholarships, but hey, sometimes in life, you gotta do what you gotta do, right? After all, taking out loans doesn't mean you are doing something wrong or failing. It just means you're taking a different path to make it work. Many people who've gone through college with loans come out just fine, just like many others who got scholarships or grants.

While taking out student loans is a common route for many, you still need to create a thoughtful strategy to manage your finances effectively and repay the loan responsibly. First and foremost, you should be aware of the many kinds of student loans. Generally, you'll encounter federal and private options, each with different interest rates and repayment terms. Federal loans, often featuring lower fixed interest rates established by the government, tend to be more advantageous for borrowers. They also offer various repayment plans, including income-driven options that tailor your monthly payments to your income level. Besides, federal loans come with certain protections, such as loan forgiveness programs for public service, options for loan consolidation, and the possibility of deferment or forbearance during financial hardship.

On the other hand, the interest rates on private student loans are usually subject to fluctuations based on the state of the market. As a result, private loan interest rates are often higher than those of federal loans. Also, they offer fewer repayment options than federal programs, which may be less flexible. Whether you're still exploring your options, have already pursued education with one of them, or are in the repayment process, remember that comprehending the interest rate and repayment terms is vital.

Even though all these discussions about interest rates and repayment terms can overwhelm you at times, the most important thing is staying on top of your loan payments. Indeed, it can feel daunting to remember that you have that student loan burden on your shoulders. However, ignoring it won't make it disappear; in fact, it can make things worse with late fees and interest piling up. It's time to face them head-on. Set up a note on your work desk or phone—whatever helps you stick with it—to remind you to keep track of your loan details and payment due dates. Taking it a step further, consider setting up automatic payments to ensure you never miss a beat.

Now, let's talk about the payment you should make each month. I know it's tempting to only pay the minimum and splurge on those fancy coffee runs or brunches, but here's the thing: By paying even a little extra each month on top of the minimum, you can chip away at the principal amount faster, saving you hundreds of dollars in interest payments in the long run. Every extra dollar you put toward your loan now is one step closer to being debt-free later on. But hey, I get it—life happens, and sometimes those extra payments just aren't in the cards. That's okay! But whenever you can, always make paying off your loans a priority, which may mean picking up a side hustle.

Paying off your student loan month by month until it's finally vanquished might seem like the only path to freedom, but fear not, fellow borrowers, for there are other alternatives to explore! There are programs that can help with loan forgiveness, wiping out your loan debt like magic. You could qualify for a loan forgiveness program known as PSLF if you have worked full-time in government or nonprofit organizations for 10 years and made 120 qualifying monthly payments. Or, if you work as a teacher who has been employed full-time in qualifying schools for 5 consecutive years, up to $17,500 of federal student loans may be forgiven, depending on qualifications (Federal Student Aid, 2022). But if you are not working in public service or as a teacher, worry not; you can still apply for an income-driven repayment (IDR) plan. Within the IDR plan, there are four programs that you may be eligible for, namely the Saving on Valuable Education (SAVE) plan, Income-Contingent Repayment (ICR) plan, Income-Based Repayment (IBR) plan, and Pay As You Earn (PAYE) plan. Based on your salary and family size, your monthly payment may be reduced, enabling simpler budget management. However, eligibility and details can vary, so do your own research and explore all your options to see what might be the best fit for your situation.

With all this talk about staying on top of payments and exploring repayment options, you might be wondering why repaying your student loan is such a big deal. Well, let me tell you, it's not just about ticking off a box or fulfilling a financial obligation. It's about setting yourself up for a future where financial freedom isn't just a dream but a reality. Keep in mind that your student loan repayment directly affects your credit score. Maintaining regular and on-time payments shows responsible credit conduct, which raises your credit score. On the other hand, neglecting repayment can significantly damage your credit score, making it harder to secure loans for your dream car or house. So, when you think about repaying your student loan, don't just see it as a chore. See it as an investment in yourself, paving the way for a future of much more affordable borrowing opportunities.

Balancing Work and Study

If you decide to work and study, whether to cover those bills, gain first-hand work experience, or bolster your resume, balancing both won't be a walk in the park. You've got work, you've got class, and on top of it all, you're trying to carve out some "me time." Indeed, it's a juggling act, and one wrong move can send everything crashing down. But fear not because it was never an impossible thing to do. Starting to balance them out means you need to set priorities and boundaries. Not all tasks are created equal. Some may be more important than others. So, take a moment before you start your day to figure out what's most important to you. Is it acing that exam you've struggled with? Is it nailing that project at work? Or is it maybe just having some downtime to recharge? Once you've defined your priorities, allocating your time and energy can be much easier.

Alongside getting your priorities straight, you need to learn about boundaries. If you're used to always saying yes, it's time to embrace the power of saying no when you need to. It's perfectly okay to turn down that extra shift or decline a last-minute invitation if it means maintaining your productivity or keeping your sanity intact. Still trying to manage your time effectively? Then, why not make technology work for you? There are tons of apps out there designed to help you manage your time better. Whether it's a calendar app to keep track of deadlines, a to-do list app to organize your tasks, or a time-tracking app to see where your time is really going, there's something out there for everyone.

Let's be honest here: Even with all your efforts to set priorities and boundaries, feeling stressed, overwhelmed, and maybe even a little burnt out from time to time is just par for the course when you're juggling work and school. It's that sensation when your body's in motion, but your mind's running on empty. The key to avoiding these feelings is by pacing yourself. I get it; having all the study and work tasks on your plate makes you want to do it all at once, but it's just a recipe for disaster. Instead, break tasks down into manageable chunks and give yourself permission to take breaks whenever you need. Think about it more like a marathon than a sprint.

Along with feeling burdened and overwhelmed, we all deal with stress. But remember, you don't have to handle this alone. Talk to someone you trust, be it a friend, relative, or even a mentor. Trust me, just venting to a friend over a coffee makes a huge difference. Or, when things go out of hand, don't be afraid to reach out and ask for help when you need it. Don't let stress get the best of you; lean on your support network when things get tough. You've got this!

Now, let's shift gears and talk about the bright side of this whole balancing act. Amidst the chaos of balancing work and study, remind yourself why you decided to do both, especially in complementing academic learning and enhancing career prospects in the future. Think about those days at your job or during your internship—sure, they might feel like added stress that other students may not have, but they're also golden opportunities to gain real-world skills that textbooks can't teach. Remember that time you aced a project at work? That's the kind of hands-on learning that sticks with you long after graduation. As an added benefit, some companies offer tuition reimbursement. So, as long as you maintain a certain GPA, your college may be paid for.

Besides the apparent cash benefit, these experiences unlock doors you might be unaware of. You'll make connections that are much wider and more relevant in your field of interest, which could lead to future job offers. Plus, you'll end up with a much stronger resume, making you stand out more when you start your career search. But how do you find these opportunities? Start talking to your network—coworkers, friends, family, and professors. They can help you identify relevant openings and connect you with their networks in your desired field. Most importantly, don't be afraid to put yourself out there—attend career fairs, scour job boards, and shoot off those cold emails.

TWO

Entering the Workforce

Isn't it just the darndest thing? Everyone around us constantly chants the "work, work, work" mantra, almost as if finding a job is the answer to all life's problems. But when it comes to actually preparing us for the real deal, it's crickets. Neither school nor college subjects seem to delve into the nitty-gritty of the working world. And what about our parents? Do they ever sit us down for a real talk about how to write a resume that doesn't look like a toddler scribbled on it or how to strut into an interview like we own the joint? And don't even get me started on the black hole of job searching. It feels like diving into an open sea without knowing where or how to start. And critical thinking? Ha! Apparently, we're supposed to magically acquire that skill along the way. Oh, and let's not forget about our rights and benefits as employees. That's like a whole other language they expect us to learn on the fly.

So yeah, maybe instead of shouting "work, work, work," they should throw in a little "learn, learn, learn," too. But fear not! Now is the time to start the talk about all the nitty-gritty you need to conquer the job market confidently. From resume writing and interviews to understanding your employee benefits, these discussions will equip you to make informed decisions, understand your rights, and land that perfect job you've always dreamt of.

Resume Writing and Job Searching

You've just wrapped up your studies, clutching that hard-earned diploma or certification in your hand. But guess what? The real world isn't going to be impressed by your academic achievements alone. Nope, that's where the resume comes into play. Think of your resume as a first impression of a potential employee even before you step foot in the door. So you better make one that has the chance to showcase your skills and talents to show employers why you're the perfect fit for the role. Sure, it might feel daunting at first, trying to condense your skills, your competence, your experience, and basically your life onto a single page, but trust me, it equips you with the most needed tool to cruise through the job search process and land that dream gig. So, what exactly is a resume, and what should it include? Essentially, a resume is a short description of your education, training, and work history. Below are the details you must consider adding to make a strong resume:

- Your contact information must be included in the resume, especially your name, address, phone number, and email address. Consider adding details such as a LinkedIn link or your website or blog if relevant to the role.

- A striking resume summary is the very first thing you should include to help the employer get a quick glimpse of your background. So, be sure to craft a compelling one that grabs their attention quickly by keeping it concise, ideally not more than three sentences, and focusing on how your skills make you the right fit.
- Your work experience(s) should be included, including any jobs you've had that were part of an apprenticeship or employment training program if you haven't had any professional job experience. List the name of the organization or company you worked for and the dates you worked there. Most importantly, briefly describe what you did in each job, and try your best to quantify your improvements or accomplishments during the work.
- Your educational background, including any relevant coursework or achievements, should include the name of the school you attended and the years you attended. Also, mention any subjects you've taken that might help you in the potential job.
- Your abilities section gives you a chance to describe other abilities about yourself that employers might find interesting, such as being bilingual, proficient in filing, working well in teams, having good writing or speaking skills, or being a fast learner.

Remember, it's not just about your hard skills; your soft skills are just as important. So, don't hesitate to let a bit of your personality shine through in your resume. After all, it's those unique traits and qualities that make you stand out from the crowd.

Most recruiters spend around eight seconds reviewing a resume, and 80% of resumes end up not getting shortlisted as they do not pass the first screen (Fennell, 2022). So, keep yours short, easy to read, and clearly organized. After all, who wants to sift through a cluttered mess of long paragraphs? Aim to keep your resume to one page and use headings, making it easier to skim and digest. Most importantly, always remember to tailor the overview of your skills to the job you're applying for. So, be sure to read the job description closely to better align your skills section. However, there is no hard and fast rule regarding the best layout for a resume, so match your layout with the personality and professionalism you want to reflect. Many websites offer free templates to help you craft that perfect resume. Before submitting it, make sure you've proofread your resume at least twice. Consider asking someone else to read through it to catch any typos, grammar errors, or writing mistakes.

Alright, so you've polished up your resume and are ready to impress employers. Now what? It's time to put those wheels in motion and find your dream job! Think of your job search like planning a road trip—you wouldn't just pick a random spot to visit, right? You'd probably ask your friends for recommendations, browse travel blogs, and check out online travel apps. So, where do you start?

First off, don't underestimate the power of networking. Tap into your connections, both online and offline, and let them know you're on the lookout for new opportunities. As your connections likely already know your work ethic and skills, you'd be surprised how fast they'd recommend you for vacancies. Then, there are online job boards such as LinkedIn, Indeed, Glassdoor, and CareerBuilder, serving as a central hub for job listings across various sectors for you to dive into. Don't be scared to cast a wide net and explore different platforms to find that perfect fit. Consider adding skills tests to your job profile. Employers will see this when viewing your resume, and it's an excellent way for you to stand out. And let's not forget about recruitment agencies swooping in to match you with your dream job. Think of them as your personal job matchmakers, in which you need to sign up first by showcasing your skills and experiences. Then, these recruitment agencies get to work, scouring their network and job listings to find roles that fit your interests and abilities. But here's the best part—once they've found a potential match, they'll hook you up with interviews, help you polish your resume, and even negotiate job offers on your behalf. Most importantly, when it comes to job searching in this digital era, be sure to spruce up your digital presence, whether on your own website or blog, social media, or LinkedIn profile. Think of them as digital business cards, showcasing your skills and experiences to potential employers.

So, you've scoured through job listings, used your network like a pro, and maybe even sought the help of recruitment agencies to land that dream job. But now comes the next step: picking out some promising opportunities and sending in your application. However, having a resume, LinkedIn profile, and portfolio isn't enough—you need to craft a compelling cover letter for your application. Think of it as your love letter to the company, ensuring you convey your passion and enthusiasm for the role. When writing a cover letter, consider which key skills and qualities you should emphasize to match the role better. But here's the thing—cover letters aren't just about restating your resume. It is your chance to inject personality into your application, to show off your passion for the role, and to let them know why you're not just another face in the crowd. If you're unsure how to write the perfect cover letter, there are many examples and templates to assist you.

You've sent off your application with your cover letter, and now you're stuck in limbo, waiting for a reply. So, how do you follow up? It's like waiting for a reply to a text—you don't want to come off as too eager, but you also don't want to be left hanging. First off, give employers some time to review your and many others' applications, probably around a week or two. After this period, a polite email or phone call can go a long way just to check in on the status of your application. Keep it short, sweet, and professional, like a friendly reminder that you're still interested in the position. If you don't hear back after your first follow-up, it's okay to send one more gentle reminder after another week or so. But beyond that, it's probably best to move on and focus your energy on other opportunities.

What if, after your initial follow-ups, they contact you, but instead of extending an interview invitation, it's a rejection? It's the bitter pill we all have to swallow, especially when it comes to job searching. Don't let it eat you up, as it's not a reflection of your worth at all. Think of it as just a temporary setback, a little bump in the road, and who knows—your dream job might just be around the corner. So, when you face rejection, dust yourself off and use this opportunity as a stepping stone for improving and refining your application or your skills for the next round.

Interview Skills and Workplace Etiquette

So, you've survived the process of making a resume, navigating follow-ups, and even weathered the storm of rejection. But now, brace yourself for actually some good news, but also the ultimate challenge at the same time: the interview invitation. Can you handle it? Indeed, being handed an interview invitation can be exhilarating yet nerve-wracking all at once. So, first, preparation is crucial in helping you feel more confident. Take a deep dive into their "About" section on the website. This section allows you to discover the products/services your potential employer offers, as well as their values, goals, and mission statement. By understanding what your employer is all about, you can better align your answers to the interview questions. Also, list questions that are likely to be asked during interviews and prepare your answers. Obviously, you'll be asked a lot about yourself and your future role, so preparing for questions related to them prevents you from feeling put on the spot. Looking up some common interview questions and reviewing the job description may help you a lot in making a potential question list. Review their job posting requirements and develop some real-life scenarios to demonstrate you have the skills they want. Consider asking friends or family to do role play to practice being interviewed.

Aside from being prepared about what to say during the interview, you must also consider how to say it. Even though it's entirely normal to feel anxious, especially in your first interview, try your best to keep calm. Be mindful of your non-verbal communication—your eye contact, gestures, and overall demeanor—as they speak volumes. They make all the difference in how employers perceive you. Most importantly, presentation matters—dress the part, show up prepared, and exude confidence. Get your clothes ready the evening before to ensure nothing goes wrong the day of. Remember, the job interview is your chance to shine, so own it like the star you are! Don't forget, 1 to 2 days after your interview, send a "thank you" email. Just sending an email thanking them for giving you the opportunity is a great way to stand out among the other prospects.

Congratulations! You've conquered the battlefield of job searching, aced the interview, and finally landed that position you applied for! But your journey is far from over. Now, it's time to navigate the maze of workplace etiquette. Working isn't just about doing your job well in the office; it's also about how you conduct yourself in a professional setting. First, let's talk about communication, as it is the lifeblood of any workplace. Ensure that your interactions, whether with your coworkers or superiors, are clear, concise, and courteous. Remember to listen as much as you speak, and always think before you convey your ideas or hit that send button on emails. Nonverbal communication is just as important, including maintaining eye contact, using appropriate hand gestures, and altering the tone of your voice. If you find yourself lacking in communication skills, fear not—you can always start by observing your senior coworkers in their interactions.

Being an employee means you'll likely be a team player, so always make sure to do your part within the deadlines. Being punctual, both in submitting your work and appearing at the office, shows your respect for your coworkers and your new responsibilities as an employee. Treat your coworkers not only as office mates but as potential allies in your career adventure. So, smile, be respectful, and maybe even bring some cookies to share because who doesn't love cookies? However, while you want to make a good impression, especially in the first few weeks or months, don't become a "yes" person. Learning to say "no" respectfully helps you create healthy boundaries while being assertive yet empathetic to others' situations.

Next up is the dress code: As a new employee, take cues from your coworkers and dress appropriately for your work environment. Whether it's business casual or corporate attire, make sure you're presenting yourself in a manner that reflects positively on you and your company. Now, onto the tricky terrain of office politics, which often feels like tiptoeing through a minefield—one wrong step and you could end up in a sticky situation. So, be diplomatic, stay neutral, and avoid getting caught up in gossip or drama. Sometimes, it's about knowing when to speak up and when to remain silent. Instead, focus on building positive relationships with your colleagues based on respect and professionalism.

So, stay in your lane and focus on ongoing learning and skill development within your new job position. Embrace new challenges, seek out opportunities to learn from coworkers, and don't be afraid to step outside your comfort zone. This continuous learning journey will not only help you excel in your current role but also prepare you for future career conquests.

Setting SMART Goals

Now, you've officially entered the thrilling world of work, where the clock on your desk ticks, emails flood in waiting to be responded to, and the coffee machine in the pantry becomes your best friend. You might think that just clocking in, doing your tasks, and making it out by 5 p.m. every day is the ticket to success in the workforce. But hold on, it's not exactly the recipe for long-term success (or, let's be honest, excitement) in the working world. That's where setting goals comes in. Without goals, you're stuck in the same loop, much like watching the same reruns year after year. It's making you closer and closer to showing up to work every day with the same "just get through the day" attitude.

On the other hand, setting goals in the world of work helps spice things up on a quest towards success both in work and your personal life. Setting goals is much like slapping a GPS onto your career path—it gives you direction, purpose, and a darn good reason to push through those Monday blues. Because in this wild world of work, it's not just about surviving; it's about thriving.

Imagine setting your goals like crafting a detailed treasure map in a sea of endless possibilities. With so many tempting opportunities swirling around, it's easy to get swept away by the currents of indecision and distraction. So, before you find yourself lost in the whirlwind of endless options, take a moment to anchor yourself with the SMART goals below.

- **Specific:** Start by honing in on exactly what you want to achieve. If your current goal as an employee is to "improve sales," make it specific: "Increase monthly sales by 10% within the next quarter." Or, if it's a vague goal of "increasing skill," specify it to "attend one professional development event every half year." Think about your passions, interests, and specific career areas you want to excel in. Not limited to your career life, being specific in setting your goals in life is a must. So start with being specific, like "save $500 per month for an emergency fund" rather than only a "save money" goal.
- **Measurable:** Make your goals quantifiable to ensure you can easily track your progress and know when you've reached the finish line. Imagine how

excited you'll be when getting closer to achieving your goals rather than having no idea where and how long the goals will be achieved. So, consider including percentage increases or decreases, dollar amounts, duration, or quantities whenever measuring your success.

- **Achievable:** Ensure your goals are realistic within the context of your role and resources when it comes to setting goals in your career life. Setting realistic goals ensures you stay motivated and avoid getting discouraged. Indeed, your goals should be challenging but, at the same time, also attainable. For example, if you're just starting your career, setting a goal to become a CEO within a year is impossible. Instead, focusing on achievable milestones like securing a leadership position within your department within a few years might be more feasible in your case.

- **Relevant:** Your goals should align with your long-term vision and aspirations. Reflect on what matters most to you and how each goal contributes to your growth and fulfillment. Or, if you are setting your career goals, ensure that the goals are aligned with the vision not only for yourself but also for your department and company. To help you determine whether your goals are relevant, ask yourself, "Does this seem worthwhile?" "Does this match my efforts?" and "Is it applicable in the current situation?" because relevant goals can answer "yes" to these questions.

- **Time-bound:** Every goal needs a deadline to create a sense of accountability and urgency. Without set deadlines, goals can easily get sidetracked by other priorities. So, determine a realistic time frame for achieving each goal and break it down into smaller milestones.

Even though you've set your SMART goals, let's face it—life has a strange way of throwing curveballs when you least expect it. No matter how meticulously you've crafted your goals, circumstances can change in the blink of an eye. It could be losing your job, company restructuring, health issues, shifting priorities, economic downturns, or even political unrest, all calling for adjustments in your goals. However, rather than seeing the need for adjustment in your goals as a sign of failure, consider it a testament to your resilience to adapt to the ever-changing nature of life. So, whenever you find yourself in circumstances that have changed, consider their impact on your original goals. Then, determine whether your existing goals remain relevant and aligned with your evolving priorities. Based on that evaluation, decide whether to stick with the original goals or establish revised goals.

Once you have your goals in hand, it should be accompanied by a tracking progress metric that allows you to track your progress objectively. Whether it's tracking sales targets, fitness milestones, or personal development achievements, having measures increases clarity and accountability throughout the progress. Grab a notebook, a whiteboard, a to-do list, a diary, or an app installed on your smartphone—

whatever works for you to visualize your progress better. If you use your phone a lot, think about installing Trello, which uses boards, lists, and cards to help you organize and prioritize tasks for multiple goals, Todoist to help you manage tasks or deadlines and track progress, or HabitHub, which gamifies goal setting to help you engage better.

For each milestone you reach, big or small, allow yourself to celebrate. Pat yourself on the back, treat yourself to something fun, indulge in a small treat you've been eyeing, share your success with loved ones, plan a weekend trip, or pursue a hobby—do what makes you happiest! Or, when you track your progress and find yourself stumbling and not making enough progress, think of it as all part of the learning process rather than beating yourself up. Reflect on the situation and identify what caused the setback. Was it something you could have controlled, or was it entirely outside your control? Consider that you may need to adjust your approach toward reaching your goals. Don't be afraid to adapt and learn from your setbacks.

Decision-Making and Critical Thinking

Stepping into adulthood and the workforce fresh out of your teenage years is undoubtedly exciting but can also feel overwhelming. It seems like you're bombarded with choices: what field to study, which job to pursue, where to live, how to manage your finances, and even what to eat. Every day presents decisions to make, from selecting a career path to handling finances. That's why being an adult calls for enhanced decision-making skills. Aside from making it easier for you to weigh pros and cons, improving decision-making skills builds confidence within you, empowering you to trust your own judgment and navigate challenges getting in your way with self-assurance. Because let's be real, nothing screams confidence like making your own decisions like the real adult you are.

Enhancing your decision-making skills starts with gathering all the information necessary to decide. Without it, you're basically flying blind! This step might involve researching different options, talking to people with experience in the field, and considering all available resources. Imagine if you're on the spot to decide whether to take on a challenging project that you haven't explored much before. You definitely need to talk to your boss about the details and expectations, research the client, and get familiar with similar projects. After you've gathered all the information, create a list of each option's potential benefits and drawbacks, allowing you to weigh the pros and cons and see the bigger picture. When you only focus on the immediate consequences, think about how today's decision might impact you in the future. Consider talking to friends, family, or mentors to hear different viewpoints on your decision. Although most might say to trust your gut, do not rely solely on your intuition. You must also combine it with the information you've gathered and the analysis you've done to make a well-informed decision. Most importantly, making good decisions takes practice. So, whenever you encounter choices, small or big, always try your best to decide on your own and gradually work your way up to more complex decisions.

Beyond improving your decision-making skills, you must also be equipped with critical thinking. As we know, the world is full of information, advice, and opinions—from news articles to social media—that are not always accurate and are sometimes misleading. Thus, critical thinking helps you sort through the noise and determine what is relevant to you. When you use critical thinking rather than making decisions based on emotion or peer pressure, you can make better decisions based on evidence and your own reasoning. Thus, developing critical thinking starts with being a questioning machine, allowing yourself to not accept information at face value. Instead, ask, "Why?" "How?" and "What if?" about everything happening around you. Then, learn to identify reliable sources and verify claims before accepting them as truth. Also, train yourself to consider multiple viewpoints on an issue by engaging in discussions with others with different opinions and trying to understand their reasoning. Whether evaluating information that comes your way or solving problems, get yourself used to relying on your critical thinking skills rather than mindlessly following the advice of others.

Understanding Employee Rights and Benefits

Hey there, new employee! Welcome to the working world! You most likely know the drill by now: show up on time, crush your tasks, and be a team player. Or if you haven't already, you'll know those things like the back of your hand in no time. But let's be honest: Do you know your rights in the workplace? Don't worry; everyone's gotta start somewhere. Most importantly, your right as an employee is to get paid for your hard work. Ensure you're getting at least the minimum wage and paid for all the hours you work. Also, you have the right to see your payslip, showing you exactly how much you earned and where any deductions went.

In every workplace or field you work in, you also have the right to work in a safe environment. That means your employer must ensure everything, like the floors, lights, and wires, are in tip-top shape. Plus, if you're working in a hazardous environment, your employer must provide the right safety gear and address any hazards promptly. So, if you ever notice that your employer isn't paying enough attention to keeping things safe, don't hesitate to speak up. After all, no one wants to show up to work every day worried about getting injured. Aside from paying attention to potential hazards, ensuring a safe environment means that your employer needs to treat all employees fairly and equally. That means no favoritism or discrimination based on race, gender, religion, or age. Just as your employer values your safety, your employer must also respect your privacy. They shouldn't be snooping into your personal stuff or sharing your private information without your consent.

As life happens, you may need a day off from work when you're feeling under the weather, need to handle something important outside of work, or even when you want to vacation. By law, you're entitled to paid time off, so use those chances to recharge, and no employer should deny you time off. Make sure you know your options for sick leave, vacation days, and other time off your employer offers. Given these basic rights as an employee laid out, if you ever find yourself in a pickle where you feel your rights are being trampled at work, don't sweat it! Check out local legal aid organizations that can offer legal assistance and advocacy tailored to your needs. Plus, don't forget about labor unions—they've got your back, too! Know you're not alone; help is just a click or call away.

Now, you've got your rights down pat, but did you know that beyond those, a whole array of employee benefits is waiting for you? On top of your salary, imagine employee benefits much like the cherry on top of your sundae—they make your work life sweeter and, eventually, your life easier. Let's start by talking about the most common employee benefit—the health insurance offered by your employer. This insurance helps cover the cost of doctor visits, prescriptions, and even hospital stays, so you can focus on getting better without stressing about the bills. Even though many employers have different policies around health insurance, generally, you are qualified for this benefit as long as you're working full-time. Along with health insurance, many employers may offer life insurance for their employees, showing that they care not only about you but also your family.

Employee benefits aren't just about meeting your immediate needs like health insurance; they're like a caring hand that supports you throughout life's journey. Not only do employers provide health insurance to keep you in top shape during your active years, but they also extend a helping hand well into your golden years. Alongside that health coverage, many employers provide you with a matching plan for your retirement account. As you put a little money from each paycheck into your retirement account, over time, with this benefit, your employer will also contribute to your account, which is essentially free money for you. Check out Chapter 4 for more details about employer-sponsored retirement plans. Aside from your insurance and matching program, your employee benefits can be paid time off, which can be used for vacation, sick days, or other personal purposes. That means you can still get paid even though you're not punching the clock. These benefits aren't just about the here and now—they are also about setting yourself up for your personal long-term success both in financial and individual well-being. So, don't just glance over the benefits package—take the time to read through every detail, like coverage limits, co-pays, and any eligibility requirements.

Understanding your rights and benefits as an employee allows you to leverage the resources available to create a work environment that supports your performance and helps you create a healthy work-life balance. Achieving this balance isn't just about clocking out on time to be with your family and friends; it's about creating a sustainable rhythm between your career and personal well-being. Thus, balancing your work and life starts with identifying what truly matters outside of work and scheduling dedicated time for them, whether it's your family, hobbies, or even self-care. Treat these appointments as seriously as work meetings because I know most of you may easily disregard the needs of these times throughout the day. If you find it hard to disconnect from work stuff after hours entirely, consider using time management apps and communication platforms with your coworkers to streamline your workflow and minimize unnecessary back and forth because, trust me, we've all been there.

Most importantly, your employer also plays a significant role in balancing your work and life, so talk openly with them about your desired work schedule and limitations. You might be surprised at how they can facilitate you further as an asset to their company, whether offering flexible work arrangements or remote work options. It is easy for us employees to hustle constantly, leaving us burned out and feeling more and more disconnected from loved ones. But once we finally prioritize setting boundaries and truly utilizing employee benefits, it'll be a game-changer. You'd be surprised at how refreshed and refocused you are when you return after getting some of your "me" time. Remember, a happy and well-rested employee is a productive employee—it's a win-win for everyone!

THREE

Mastering Money Basics

A h, welcome to Adulting 101, where we dive headfirst into the thrilling world of managing our own finances! Budgeting, saving for the future, and, oh yes, let's not forget everyone's favorite pastime—filing taxes! It's like being dropped into a foreign country where they speak a language made up entirely of financial jargon. And don't even get me started on the joy of deciphering terms like interest rates, credit scores, and tax brackets. It's enough to make you want to pull your hair out.

Sure, we weren't exactly handed a manual on how to navigate this financial jungle in school. Also, we're expected to figure it out on our own and somehow thrive in it. But hey, we're in this together! Many young adults, just like you, are sailing in the same leaky boat, trying to make sense of our finances while juggling a million other things. Trust me, everyone has had their moments of feeling utterly lost when it comes to money matters.

So, if you're feeling overwhelmed or clueless, just remember: it's all part of the learning process. And hey, don't wallow in that sea of confusion for too long. Use this chapter as a compass to help guide you through budgeting, saving, using credit cards without maxing them out, and even tackling those dreaded tax forms.

Budgeting Like a Boss: Crafting a Personal Budget That Works for You

Picture yourself trekking through a place you've never been to without a map or compass. You'd feel lost, frustrated, and like you're going in circles, even when you think you're making progress. Your financial journey is a bit like that—complex and intimidating—without you setting your goals first. Whether paying off student loans, saving for your dream car, buying a home, or securing your child's future, having clear financial goals is like having a roadmap to guide you. It helps you focus on what's important and take meaningful steps toward making your dreams a reality. By painting a picture of your future, you can start taking actionable steps today to get there.

When you think about your financial goals, do you ever catch yourself saying things like, "I want to be loaded," "I want to have enough cash to do whatever I want," "I want to save more money," or "I want to retire comfortably"? Totally normal! But those vague goals won't get you far. Instead, let's get honest about what you really want and break it down into smaller, doable steps. Instead of just saying "save more," think about specifics like "cutting back on spending by 10%

next month" or "putting $150 into savings each paycheck." Keep your goals aligned with your current financial situation. Unrealistic goals can bum you out and make you feel like you'll never get there. So, swap out that "become a millionaire" dream for something like "boost my income by 10% in the next three months." It's all about building confidence and keeping your eyes on the prize!

Once you've sorted your goals, it's time to put a timeframe on them. No more wishy-washy "someday" or "in the future" vibes—let's get specific! Sort your goals into groups based on their duration—short and long-term. Short-term goals address immediate needs that can be achieved within a few months to a few years, such as saving for a vacation, building an emergency fund, paying off credit card debt, or purchasing a new electronic device. On the other hand, long-term objectives, like buying your dream house, accumulating an investment portfolio, launching a business, or preparing for retirement, provide you with direction for your financial future and call for consistent effort over years to decades. Aim for that sweet spot between "too easy" and "way too hard"—kinda like walking a tightrope. You wanna be challenged, but not so much that you feel like giving up.

So, you've got your short-term and long-term goals all sorted out. Now, answer these two questions: "How much comes in?" and "How much goes out?" But don't worry, it's not as scary as it sounds!

First up, let's figure out how much money you're bringing in. Besides your main job, are you hustling on the side, freelancing, or dabbling in some entrepreneurial ventures?

In today's gig economy, it's pretty common to have multiple income streams. So, jot down all your income sources—your salary, side gig earnings, bonuses, commissions, you name it. Then, note how often you get paid—weekly, bi-weekly, or monthly. This way, you'll have a clear picture of your monthly income. Knowing this helps you budget better so you don't accidentally overestimate or underestimate your expenses. If you're freelancing, running your own business, or making money through tips, hourly gigs, or commissions, figuring out your average monthly income is a bit trickier. But don't worry, just start gathering up all the cash coming your way over the past three or six months and add it all together. Then, divide that total by the number of months you're looking at. Voila! You've got your average monthly income.

Now, let's talk about where your money goes. After you cash your paycheck, you've probably got your fixed costs covered —rent, utilities, groceries. But what about the rest? If you're not sure where your money's disappearing, it's time to start tracking your expenses. List every single expense, big or small. From rent to that latte you grabbed on the go, record it all. Then, categorize your expenses—housing, groceries, dining out, utilities, transportation, entertainment, you name it. Tracking and categorizing your expenses gives you a peek into your spending habits and patterns, showing where your money's going and where you might be able to cut back a bit.

After you've figured out your average monthly income and expenses, it's time to allocate the right amount of money for each budget category. There's no one-size-fits-all method for this—it's all about finding what suits you best. So, be open to experimenting with different approaches that match your lifestyle and spending habits. Feeling overwhelmed with where to start? Well, this popular rule called the 50/30/20 rule might be worth a shot.

Here's the gist of it: Half of your income—that's 50%—should cover your essential expenses like rent, groceries, bills, and insurance. You know, the stuff you can't really live without. This chunk ensures you can keep your head above water without stressing too much about money. Then comes the fun part—the 30%. This slice of your earnings is all about treating yourself. Whether it's dining out, picking up a new hobby, or jetting off on a weekend getaway, this is your guilt-free spending money. It's about enjoying life without feeling like you're pinching pennies at every turn. Last but not least, there's the 20% set aside for savings and paying off debts. It's not the most glamorous part, but it's crucial for building a more stable financial foundation. Think of it as investing in your future self—whether that's building an emergency fund, saving up for a big purchase, or paying down those pesky credit card bills. So, with the 50/30/20 rule, you're striking a balance between taking care of your needs, indulging in some wants, and securing your financial future. It's a simple yet effective way to manage your money and work towards your goals without feeling like you're constantly juggling your finances.

Aside from allocating what portion of your income goes to each category of your expenses, budgeting is all about finding that one method that encourages you to stick with it consistently. Consider your personality and preferences so you can better align them with a particular budgeting method. Ask yourself, "Am I more detail-oriented, or do I prefer a more relaxed approach?" and "Do I prefer cash or cashless spending?" While some find digital transactions more convenient, others may think that physically seeing the money leave their wallet makes it simpler to stay within a budget.

For many of us tech-savvy adults, diving into the world of digital budgeting apps just makes sense. Apps like Mint, Rocket Money, YNAB (You Need a Budget), and PocketGuard offer a digital playground for tracking expenses, setting budgets, and even categorizing transactions automatically from your bank accounts. It's like having a personal finance assistant in your pocket—perfect for those of us glued to our phones 24/7. With these apps, you can set spending limits for different categories and get real-time updates on where your money is going. Plus, they're super handy for keeping tabs on your finances without digging through receipts.

But hey, if you like to keep things old school, there's always a spreadsheet for budgeting or the trusty envelope budgeting method. With this method, you divide your cash into different envelopes, each labeled with a specific expense category—groceries, gas, entertainment, you name it. When the money runs out in one envelope, that's it—no more spending in that category until the next month rolls around. It's like having a physical reminder of your budget right there in your wallet. And let's be honest, there's something oddly satisfying about physically handing over cash for your purchases—it makes you really think twice about where your money's going.

Whether you've implemented budgeting through using a conventional or digital budgeting method, it's not the end of the road. Life has a way of throwing curveballs, and as our circumstances change, so too must our budgeting plan. You should regularly reassess and adjust your budgeting strategy, whether it's on a monthly, quarterly, or semi-annual basis. Consider revisiting your budget whenever you experience significant life changes, such as shifts in income due to job changes, promotions, or loss of income, as well as major life events like getting married, having children, or shifting priorities. Any change, no matter how tiny, might affect your financial situation and force you to modify your budgeting strategy. Not only should you update your budget to account for any recent changes in your current situation, but doing so on a regular basis may also show you where you can make savings and reallocate money. This proactive approach ensures that your budget remains aligned with your current needs and goals, setting you up for financial success in the long haul.

Navigating the World of Credit Cards: Using Them Wisely to Build Your Future

Mastering the basics of managing money as an older teen or young adult like you often involves a whirlwind of juggling newfound financial responsibilities, whether it's paying rent, buying groceries, or occasionally treating yourself to that concert ticket or a stylish outfit for upcoming parties. It's exhilarating to purchase things that your parents previously might not have approved of, isn't it? But as reality sets in, you might wonder how to foot those bills while relying only on your income. That's where the magic of credit cards comes into play—a small rectangular piece of plastic that lets you swipe and enjoy life's pleasures right before your eyes. As someone who's been in the complexities of adulthood myself, I understand the allure of credit cards. But getting your first credit card isn't just about convenient transactions—it's about dealing with the world of building credit and managing debt.

Given the perks and pitfalls of credit cards, before applying for your first, ensure you familiarize yourself with its basics. First and foremost, let's talk about interest rates—the sneaky little numbers determining how much extra you'll pay if you carry a balance on your card from month to month. The more often you carry a balance, the more interest you incur over time and the longer it will take you to pay off what you owe. Therefore, ensuring you're aware of these rates saves you lots of money and prevents you from accumulating debt faster. Next up, minimum payments: The bare minimum you need to pay each month to keep your account in good standing. It might seem manageable at first to only pay the minimum amount, but keep in mind that interest keeps racking up, making you end up owing more than you originally spent. Thus, think about minimum payment only as a lifeline when funds are tight and aim for more than minimum whenever possible to chip away your balance faster.

Other than choosing a credit card that is most suitable for your finances, being aware of its interest rate and minimum payment contributes a lot to your credit scores in the future. After all these unfamiliar phrases of interest rate and minimum payment, you might wonder what a credit score is or why it is even important. Your credit score is basically a snapshot of your creditworthiness, influencing everything from the interest rates you'll be offered to the likelihood of securing loans or renting an apartment on more favorable terms. In this sense, a high credit score is basically your golden ticket to navigating adulthood because it makes it easier for you to obtain the loans you've always needed, to get an affordable mortgage to purchase your dream home, lowers your insurance costs, and even helps you land the job of your dreams. Numerous benefits come with having a good score, making it seem as if luck and good fortune are on your side while, in reality, they are the product of your own conscious efforts. So, as tempting as it is to max out your credit limit on that impulse buying, resist that urge as much as possible. Instead, start small and only charge what you can afford to pay off in full each month to demonstrate responsible credit usage better. Then, make it a priority to pay your credit card on time, every time. Consider setting a reminder to ensure you never miss a due date.

However, what happens if you've already accrued debt from late payments, which lowers your credit score? No worries. Your credit score might be low right now, but you can increase it a step at a time. So, first things first, resist the urge to keep swiping—that is like pouring gasoline on a fire. Just stop making the transaction against your credit card and focus on getting out of the hole you're in. Then, refer back to your budgeting and identify areas where you can cut back to allocate more toward your accumulated debt. If you're still struggling to maximize debt payment, look for ways to bring in extra income, like freelance jobs, online gigs, or even selling unused items. Keep in mind that you should allocate every extra cent toward paying down that debt. With a little sacrifice and more hard work, you can conquer that debt and get back to using your credit card responsibly.

However, to avoid getting into that debt hole anymore, you need to watch out for payday loans. They might seem like a quick fix when you're strapped for cash, but they often come with sky-high interest rates. Remember that those "easy money" solutions often come with hidden costs that can leave you worse off than before. So, how do you dodge these debt traps? Well, like many others, knowledge is power! Whether you're considering taking out a personal loan, financing a big purchase, or applying for a new credit card, make sure you understand precisely what you're going into. Remind yourself not to rush and choose blindly; take your time and read thoroughly the fine print, especially about the interest rates, fees, and repayment terms. It might not be the most thrilling read, but trust me, it's much better than getting hit with unexpected fees or finding yourself locked into a contract you can't afford.

The Essentials of Saving: Strategies for Growing Your Safety Net—Banking Essentials

Having your own income means it's time to step up your money game—paying bills, managing expenses, and keeping track of your hard-earned cash. And that's where a checking account becomes your new best friend, replacing that old piggy bank at home. No more worrying about losing your cash; a checking account has got your back. It's not just a safe place to stash your money; it's a way to make it grow a little with interest. Plus, it's way more convenient for your everyday transactions. Who wants to carry around wads of cash everywhere? With a checking account, you can pay bills online, swipe your debit card for snacks, or even Venmo your friend for that late-night pizza run. Everything you need is right at your fingertips, making life a whole lot easier.

But wait, there's more! A checking account serves as the ropes of money management, where you can see how much you have, track your spending patterns, and avoid going overboard on impulse buys. So yeah, getting a checking account might seem like a small step, but it's a giant leap into the world of adulting. For tech-savvy adults, checkbook apps are highly recommended. You can even set bill reminders on them.

With all these banks and account options out there, it can feel overwhelming to start choosing one. But fear not! Let's break it down a bit and talk about the factors you should consider to help you pick the right one.

- **Fees:** Nobody likes surprise charges eating into their hard-earned cash. So, make sure you know what you're getting into upfront. Whether it's monthly fees, annual fees, or other sneaky charges, be aware of them. Account maintenance and minimum balance fees are the most common with checking accounts. While an account maintenance fee covers ongoing account management, a minimum balance fee is incurred only if your balance drops below the required minimum. Thus, always ensure you maintain at least the minimum balance in your account. If you rely on those cash machines, you should be aware that your bank may charge you for ATM fees if you use an ATM that is not affiliated with your bank's network, ranging up to a few dollars per transaction. But, if you want to avoid ATM fees, choose a bank that offers reimbursement for network withdrawal fees as one of the benefits or plan your withdrawals in advance. Plus, in a checking account, an overdraft fee is imposed only when you spend more than your balance, ranging from $10 to $35. To avoid overdraft fees, you should monitor your account activity not only to ensure your balance does not fall below a certain amount but also to track your spending habits and identify areas where you can cut back. Or, setting up alerts on your account for low balances or large transactions can help you stay aware of your financial situation in real-time, allowing you to take action before overdrafts occur. With all these standard fees, make sure you balance out your banking needs while minimizing fees as much as possible. Remember that different bank and account types come with different fee structures, so contact your bank representative to know more. Some banks offer young adult accounts with lower or no fees, so be on the lookout for those.

- **Service:** Trust is key when it comes to choosing a bank. You want peace of mind knowing your money is in good hands. So, do a quick internet scan to check for any recent security breaches. And since we're all glued to our phones these days, find a bank with a user-friendly mobile app that lets you check balances, transfer funds, and even deposit checks with just a snap—all without stepping foot in a branch. And hey, if you're all about that digital life, consider an online bank, as they often have lower fees and higher interest rates.

- **Interest rates**: While checking accounts typically don't offer much in the way of interest, it is still worth comparing rates between different banks to make sure you're getting the best deal possible.

While a checking account is great for everyday stuff like getting groceries, morning coffee, or buying things at the store, you should also consider opening a savings account. Think about it as a piggy bank but on steroids. Instead of letting your cash float around your wallet or checking account, tempting you with every sale you encounter, a savings account safely stores your money with a little bonus just for keeping your money there—known as interest, which is much bigger than in a checking account. Indeed, the interest rate in a savings account won't make you a millionaire overnight, but those little bumps add up over time, making your savings goals even more achievable. With money saved in a savings account, when you want to spend your savings on a dream vacation, a new phone, or a concert ticket, you've got your money ready without feeling the pinch.

However, getting used to saving habits is not only about discretionary spending but also about setting aside money for big-ticket items like your car down payment, buying your own cozy home, or a comfortable retirement. It's not just about having them at your hand; think about it as investing in your dreams. And trust me, there's something incredibly empowering about watching those savings grow, knowing that each dollar brings you one step closer to your goal. Sure, that new gadget or fancy vacation might seem pretty tempting at the moment, but think about the satisfaction of achieving something bigger down the line. Imagine the next 5, 10, and 15 years from now. No one will bring those dreams to your lap but yourself.

So, how can you start setting aside money for these significant future expenses? First, figure out the estimated amount you need to save and set a deadline. Based on the deadline, you should break the amount down into smaller, manageable chunks. That way, you know a certain amount from each paycheck needs to be allocated or cut back on non-essentials for a while until the target is reached. Trust me, it is worth the sacrifice. Also, remember to celebrate every milestone you've passed to give yourself a pat on the back. Acknowledge that you're making moves, and that's something to be proud of. Indeed, saving for big future purchases might not be as flashy as owning a sports car or taking a cruise vacation in Hawaii, but you're on your way to unlocking the life you've always dreamed of.

And let's not overlook the peace of mind that comes with having savings and being prepared for whatever life throws your way. Building savings also means having an emergency fund on hand, where you set aside money from your regular expenses in a dedicated cash reserve for unexpected financial emergencies. Think of it as a safety net that protects you from life's curveballs, which, let's face it, often catch you off guard. With your emergency fund in place, you don't have to stress about scrambling for high-interest loans or maxing out your credit cards when emergencies pop up. Whether it's a busted phone, a surprise medical bill, or a sudden car repair, you've got it covered without dipping into your long-term savings or piling up debt. Now, without that emergency fund? Even the smallest financial hiccup could throw a wrench in your plans and leave you drowning in debt. That's why, ideally, you need to aim for at least three to six months' worth of living expenses stashed away. It's your safety net, providing a buffer to bounce back from any financial emergencies. Even if you're still dealing with irregular income, student loans, or navigating tough times, every dollar you save toward your emergency fund counts. So, make it a habit to tuck away a little something, even when money's tight.

Whether you're stashing cash for those unexpected rainy days or saving up for that dream vacation, you want to pick a savings account that's got your back and helps your money grow. Here's a rundown of some savings accounts you might want to consider:

- **Traditional Savings Accounts**: This is the most basic account, simple to understand, and usually offered by conventional banks. They're great for starting out because they often don't have any fees to open, but the interest rates might not make you jump for joy. Still, they're a safe bet, especially if you're just dipping your toes into the world of saving. Just watch out for those sneaky monthly maintenance fees and limits on how many times you can take money out.

- **High-Yield Savings Accounts (HYSA):** These offer a more competitive interest rate on savings compared to traditional savings accounts. HYSAs are often offered by online banks to attract people who want to earn a better rate than what's available at brick-and-mortar banks. Thus, HYSA is an ideal option for saving for bigger goals that won't need immediate access to the money. Just keep an eye on any minimum balance requirements and make sure you're okay with potentially fewer ways to access your cash.

- **Money Market Accounts (MMAs):** With MMAs, you may make out checks or use a debit card and still earn interest, combining the greatest features of savings and checking accounts. Yet, MMAs usually allow a limited number of monthly withdrawals, maintaining their status as a saving rather than a transactional tool. Also, MMAs often offer higher interest rates in return for higher minimum balance requirements. However, the interest rates tend to fluctuate depending on market conditions, which brings a degree of risk compared to other savings accounts. Thus, MMAs are suitable for those seeking higher interest while maintaining some level of liquidity.

There is no one-size-fits-all solution, so find your own sweet spot that helps your hard-earned cash grow without annoying restrictions. Once you've sorted out which savings account suits you best, it's time to kickstart your savings game with some personalized tricks. First, set up automatic transfers from your paycheck straight into your savings account. Think of it as treating your future self to a little bonus before you even get tempted to spend it, ensuring you're always making progress without even thinking about it.

Alongside automatic transfers, track your spending triggers to become aware of those sneaky habits that cause you to whip out your wallet without realizing it. We all have them—maybe it's the boredom that leads to endless scrolling on your favorite e-commerce site, the plan to dine out that sparks a spree of trendy clothes purchases or the daily latte habit that adds up over time. Identifying these triggers is critical to plugging up those money leaks and being mindful of your spending habits. Once you know what they are, you can come up with strategies to outsmart them to fend off unnecessary spending. By staying mindful of your triggers and setting up automatic transfers, you'll be able to make intentional choices about where your money goes, ensuring you're not just spending but saving for the things that truly matter to you.

Understanding Taxes: What You Need to Know and How to File Them

Now that you're working, have you ever wondered where a big chunk of your hard-earned cash disappears every month? Let's face it: managing your finances as you approach adulthood includes more than simply setting up credit cards, saving money, and creating a budget. You also have to pay taxes. It's about realizing where a significant portion of your hard-earned money goes each month. Getting a grip on money basics requires you to unlock the secrets of the tax system, making it less confusing and maybe even saving you some cash in the process.

So, before diving into the nitty-gritty of tax documents or filing taxes, what exactly are taxes? Essentially, taxes are mandatory fees imposed by the government on you as a citizen to fund public expenditures. Picture taxes as the fuel that powers essential services and infrastructure like roads, schools, hospitals, and emergency services. Think about how you can cruise around town comfortably because of smooth roads, how you've learned all the knowledge you have so far from schools, how you have free places to hang out in parks or libraries, and how safe your area is because of police and firefighters. By paying taxes, you're basically investing in your community, ensuring that it remains a safe, prosperous, and well-functioning place to live. So, taxes aren't just about parting ways with your money; they're about collectively pooling resources to build and sustain the society we all rely on.

Navigating the maze of taxes can feel overwhelming, especially when you realize you're on the hook for both federal and state taxes. Federal taxes cover a broad spectrum of areas, including income tax, payroll tax, and corporate tax. The national government imposes these taxes for national stuff like defense, social security, and maybe even funding that cool space program. These taxes have set rates across the country, so no matter where you live, you'll pay the same percentage of federal tax based on your income bracket. Meanwhile, unlike federal taxes, states also impose taxes on sales, property, and sometimes even inheritance. State taxes are imposed by individual states for things like fixing potholes on your local roads, funding your high school, or even maintaining that beach you've loved to hang out at for years. Thus, these rates of taxes may vary depending on where you live. Some states have a flat rate, meaning everyone pays the same percentage, while others have a progressive system, where high earners pay a bigger chunk. Understanding the difference between federal and state taxes isn't just about numbers and percentages; it's about grasping how these taxes impact your daily life. Federal taxes might seem distant, but they still shape the national landscape, which affects us all. Meanwhile, state taxes hit closer to home, literally, as they fund services and infrastructure right in your neighborhood.

After understanding the contrast between federal and state taxes, delving into the world of taxes means grasping the significance of W-2s and 1099s. Your W-2s are what your employer provides you at the end of the year about precisely how much you've earned and how much tax has been deducted from your paycheck along the way. It's like your job's way of saying, "Hey, here's what you made this year, and here's what we owe the government on your behalf." On the flip side, the 1099 comes into play when you've earned income outside your primary job, such as through freelancing gigs or interest on investments. It gives a gentle nudge, showing, "Hey, you've earned some cash outside your regular job, and now it's time to pay up." These forms tell the government exactly how much money you earn throughout the year. That way, the government can calculate your tax bill accurately. Thus, familiarizing yourself with W-2s and 1099s lays the groundwork for navigating tax documentation.

Now that we've wrapped our heads around your W-2s and 1099s, the next step is piecing them together to complete the picture—filing our taxes. When it comes to filing taxes, you've got options! The first choice, of course, is to tackle it yourself online. There are plenty of user-friendly websites and software out there, like TurboTax, H&R Block, and TaxAct, that guide you through the process step by step. These platforms ensure you can easily input your information and file taxes electronically. Or, if your income falls below a certain threshold, you could be eligible for the IRS Free File Program, which lets you prepare and submit your federal taxes for free using online software offered by reputable businesses.

However, if the thought of doing your taxes alone gives you a bit of anxiety, don't worry. You've got another option: seeking professional help. You can enlist the expertise of a tax preparer or accountant who knows all the ins and outs of the tax code. They'll ask you for your documents, sort through them, and ensure everything is done correctly. Whether you opt for DIY online filing or seek professional assistance, the most important thing is to ensure your taxes are filed on time. Don't think about it as a difficult thing to do, which only makes things feel harder and overwhelming. Think about it like ripping off a band-aid—you just gotta do it, and then you can move on with your life. Taxes can be tricky, but with a little patience and maybe a cup of coffee or two, you'll get through it just fine. You got this!

Not limited to accuracy, filing taxes is also about finding ways to reduce that bill a bit. In addition to your W-2s and 1099s, try your best to gather evidence of deductions, such as receipts for charitable donations, student loan interest payments, or medical expenses—whatever applies to your situation. These documents enable you to subtract from your taxable income, ultimately reducing your overall tax bill.

In addition to deductions, you might also benefit from tax credits. Think of tax deductions like using a coupon that takes a percentage off your total grocery bill, while tax credits are more like finding a surprise $10 bill in your wallet while paying for groceries. While a deduction reduces your taxable income by a percentage, a tax credit lowers your tax liability dollar for dollar.

For adults like you, there are specific credits you might qualify for. If you're still in college, you might be eligible for the American Opportunity Tax Credit to offset some of your education expenses. Or, if you're a low to moderate-income earner, you might qualify for the Earned Income Tax Credit

(EITC). To find out what tax deductions and credits apply to you, refer to the IRS website or consult tax preparation software or a tax professional. It's all about ensuring you take advantage of every opportunity to save money on your taxes and keep more hard-earned cash in your pocket.

FOUR

Investing in Your Future

I magine this: In the future, you will be chilling on a beach with a drink in hand or waiting to start your journey traveling around the world, thanking your younger self for being a total rockstar. How do you achieve that? It's all by investing in your future. You are succeeding in ditching those instant gratifications and saving money for your future by investing in stocks, bonds, and mutual funds. These are tools to grow your money over time, thanks to something magical called compound interest. It's like earning interest on your interest, making your money snowball into a financial fortune. Plus, when you decide to invest in that mysterious cryptocurrency everyone's talking about, you're basically supercharging your money. The younger you start, the more time this snowball of investments has to work, so let's get you set up to get that beach-bumming future you deserve!

Starting Small: Intro to Investing for Young Adults

With today's fast-paced economy and high inflation rates, relying solely on saving simply won't cut it anymore. Sure, putting money aside is a good start, but if you want to really supercharge your financial future, now is the time to shift gears and dive into the world of investing. Now, I know what you're thinking—with education costs, housing expenses, and everyday bills piling up, who has the luxury to think about investing, right? And let's not forget about those pesky student loans or credit card debts adding to the mix. But here's the thing—investing doesn't have to mean diving in with hundreds of dollars or sacrificing your essentials. Even if it's just a tiny percentage of your income, investing in your 20s can set you up for success in ways you wouldn't believe. Think of it as planting the seeds for a bountiful financial garden. The earlier you start, the longer your money has to grow, thanks to the magic of compound interest. Plus, starting early means you can afford to take more risks, spice things up, and aim for those bigger returns that might just change your life. So why wait? Your future self is counting on you to make the smart move today.

Not quite sure where to kickstart your investing journey? Well, get ready for a wild ride! Whether you're a risk-taking junkie or a cautious penny pincher, there's always an option for everyone. Below are the investment options worth considering for beginners like you.

- **Stocks** enable you, as a stockholder, a slice of ownership in the company. Think of stocks as tiny portions of ownership in companies you love, like that cutting-edge tech company where you snagged your latest gadget or the trendy fashion brand you swear by. When that company thrives, you're entitled to a share of its assets and earnings, known as dividends. It's like being part of the company's team, but it also means there's a chance that your stock's value will dip when the company faces financial struggles. Apart from depending on the company's performance, your stock's value can also be influenced by economic conditions and global events, adding an extra layer of unpredictability.

- **Bonds** are essentially loaning money to big organizations, whether it's a government or a corporation. In return, they promise to pay you back with interest at the end of the term. While government bonds are generally considered safer, bonds issued by individual companies can carry more risk, especially if the company faces financial struggles. However, compared to stocks, bonds offer a safer option, which also comes with much lower returns. Bonds might not be as flashy as stocks, but they sure know how to keep your investment portfolio sailing smoothly.

- **Mutual funds** combine a diverse mix of assets, including stocks, bonds, and sometimes even real estate, by pooling everyone's money together. Rather than investing in individual stocks, mutual funds offer more diversified portfolios that can spread your risk better. Compared to managing your own portfolio, mutual funds are a powerful financial vehicle that can withstand any storm. Choosing specific investments for your portfolio and monitoring market conditions take time and effort, but investing in mutual funds saves you both. However, keep in mind that as a fund manager handles mutual funds, you'll need to pay fees, which can occasionally add up. Also, some mutual funds may require a certain minimum investment amount.

When making decisions about allocation in stocks, bonds, and mutual funds, your risk tolerance, or the amount of risk you can and will tolerate, should be taken into account, as well as your investment goals. Remember, the higher the risk you take, the greater the potential returns, but also the greater the chance of losing your hard-earned money. So, if you have a higher risk tolerance and are aiming for long-term growth, you might feel comfortable with a more aggressive investment strategy, which includes a higher allocation to stocks in your portfolio. On the flip side, if you have a lower risk tolerance or are investing for short-term goals, you might prefer a more conservative approach, with a greater emphasis on bonds or mutual funds. It's all about finding that sweet spot between risk and returns to build a well-diversified investment portfolio.

Once you've learned more about your risk tolerance and investment goals, your next step is to decide between using a robo-advisor or a traditional brokerage firm to manage your investments. Robo-advisors are automated investment platforms that utilize algorithms to construct and oversee a diversified portfolio tailored to your unique preferences. To set up a robo-advisor account, you'll typically complete an online questionnaire to assess your risk tolerance and investment objectives. From there, the robo-advisor will recommend a portfolio suited to your needs. These platforms are incredibly user-friendly, making them perfect for beginner investors seeking a hands-off approach, but they also come with limited investment options. Notable robo-advisor platforms worth considering include Betterment, Vanguard Digital Advisor, and SoFi Automated Investing.

On the other hand, traditional brokerage firms offer a broader range of investment options and services, including access to individual stocks, bonds, mutual funds, and more. Opening an account with a traditional broker usually involves filling out an application online or in person and funding your account with an initial deposit. The downside? You'll need to conduct research and make your own investment decisions. If you enjoy closely monitoring your portfolio and actively participating in the day-to-day decision-making process of buying and selling investments, opening a traditional brokerage account may be ideal for you.

Regardless of the type of account you're considering, you must be mindful of minimum balance requirements, fees, and other pricing schedules as you move forward. If you are a conservative investor with limited money to get started, look for accounts with no minimum balance requirements. On the other hand, if you opt for a more aggressive approach with a specific type of brokerage account, you may need thousands of dollars to get started. Also, when deciding which account to open, review the services offered, such as mobile trading, foreign trading options, and stock ratings, to determine whether they suit your needs. Once you've decided on the platform or brokerage company that best suits your preferences, to complete the application process, you might need to provide personal and documentation details, such as your name, driver's license, passport, or other official government identification, social security number, birth date, address, phone number, email address, and details on your employment status. In some instances, details regarding your net worth, annual income, risk tolerance, and investment goals may also be required.

As you finish your investment account application, it doesn't guarantee immediate returns once you start investing. Instead, your investments may likely decrease in value in the short term. It might be tempting to react to market ups and downs and feel discouraged, but remember, you're playing the long game here. Think of it like planting a seed—you wouldn't pull it up every day to see if it's sprouted, would you? Remember that time is key when it comes to letting your investments grow. The longer you hold onto your investments, the less those ups and downs matter. Thus, to prevent yourself from being anxious about market fluctuations, consider setting up regular contributions to your account to remove the temptation to time the market and encourage disciplined investing habits.

Retirement Accounts Unveiled: Understanding Your 401(k) and IRA Options

Finally getting to trade in your work suit for comfy PJs while spending 24/7 with loved ones and spending your days exactly how you please; no more being anxious about whether your day off or vacation will be approved or not because you have all the time in the world—now, that's the dream retirement scenario, right? As much as we have always dreamed of this kind of retirement, when it comes to reality, no one seems to know exactly how to achieve it. In the US alone, more than half of Americans have not saved enough money throughout their working years to pay for their daily needs in retirement, let alone fulfilling their dreams of traveling around the world or cruising while visiting tropical islands (Transamerica Center for Retirement Studies, 2022). In turn, four out of ten Americans say they intend to work past the retirement age. So, are you one of those who plan to stay working even after retirement? Can you guarantee you can still work properly and meet your boss's expectations in your 60s?

Therefore, start saving for your retirement before you're grey and old. Indeed, it's easy to think, "Retirement? That's ages away. I'll worry about it later." But here's the fact: The earlier you start saving, even a little bit each paycheck, the more time your money has to work its magic. Think about how much less of a dent it puts in your wallet now, rather than waiting until your 40s or 50s, when retirement is looming. Also, starting retirement saving at your age means you have decades ahead to let your investments ride the waves of the market, weathering the ups and downs along the way. Plus, again and again, compound interest will help you accumulate your retirement savings as the returns generated over time. It's like a snowball rolling down a hill, gathering momentum and getting bigger and bigger over time. And let's not forget about those sweet, sweet tax advantages. By stashing away money in retirement accounts like a 401(k) or IRA, you're not only building your nest egg but also potentially lowering your tax bill. It's like getting a double win for your future self! Sure, saving for retirement for decades away might mean sacrificing a bit of instant gratification now and then, from skipping fancy brunch or cutting back on those impulse buys, but think about how those "losses" can transform into that tropical vacation without a care in the future.

Then, how should you allocate a percentage of your monthly income toward your retirement needs? Retirement savings accounts are the answer. Though there is a vast array of these accounts to select from, below are the most commonly used ones with their pros and cons. Securing your future isn't just about crunching numbers; it's about finding the perfect fit for your preferences and financial circumstances.

401(k) Plans

401(k) plans are employer-sponsored retirement savings plans that are part of their benefits package. However, even though these plans are employer-sponsored, if you decide to leave your current job, you can transfer your retirement savings either to your new employer or into your own IRA account. These plans typically contain prerequisites for eligibility, including a certain amount of hours worked each week or a minimum length of service. Enrolling in a 401(k) plan entails consenting to contribute a portion of your earnings toward retirement automatically. Your 401(k) plans' combined funds are then invested in a range of securities, usually stocks, bonds, and mutual funds. However, with a 401(k) plan, you may have limited investment options available. In most cases, your employer or plan administrator may choose a set of investments for your retirement account.

Aside from your regular payments to the 401(k) plan, most employers may offer employer matching. Have you ever heard of employer matching? Or do you recognize that your current employer now offers employer matching? Employer matching refers to the process by which your company matches your annual contribution to your retirement savings up to a certain sum or percentage; practically, it's free money for you. Who doesn't want free money, right? So, to maximize the benefits of employer matching, consider consulting with your HR department to be aware of specific policies and options available for your retirement plan because employer matching varies depending on your employer. If your employer offers dollar-for-dollar matching up to 5% of your salary, you should contribute at least 5% of your salary to your 401(k) to maximize the match. Alternatively, if your employer offers partial matching, aim to contribute at least the percentage of your salary that your employer matches. For instance, if your employer matches 50% of your contributions up to 6% of your salary, aim to contribute 6% to maximize the match. Consider setting up automatic contributions from your paycheck to ensure you make the most of your employer matching and don't miss out on any matching funds.

Individual Retirement Account (IRA) Plans

While 401(k) plans are typically employer-sponsored, IRAs are individual retirement savings accounts that you can open and manage on your own as long as you earn income. That way, unlike with 401(k) programs, you have to open and fund your own IRA account without receiving company matching funds. You can register and contribute to an IRA even if your employer already offers a 401(k) plan. Thus, opening an IRA is a smart move if you're worried that your retirement savings from your 401(k) might not be enough. Furthermore, compared to 401(k) plans, IRAs can be the better option for you if you wish to invest your retirement savings in a greater variety of financial instruments, such as stocks, bonds, mutual funds, and exchange-traded funds (ETFs).

Both 401(k) and IRA retirement savings plans can be divided into the two types below.

- With **a traditional savings plan**, you contribute money from your paycheck before taxes are taken out, reducing your taxable income for the year. That way, you get a bigger paycheck now, which is pretty sweet for that weekend getaway or your favorite artist's concert you've been eyeing. As your investments grow without being taxed until you withdraw them in retirement, traditional savings plans allow them to grow faster. But here's the catch: When you finally retire, you'll owe taxes on the money you withdraw as ordinary income. When it comes to withdrawal rules, with a traditional savings plan, starting at age 72, you must take out a certain amount each year, subjecting you to potential tax implications. Failure to do so can result in hefty penalties.

- On the other hand, contributions made to **a Roth savings plan** are made after taxes are deducted from your salary, so they do not reduce your annual taxable income. However, all qualifying retirement withdrawals, including investment earnings, are tax-free. In contrast to traditional savings plans, Roth savings plans do not have lifetime minimum payout requirements, enabling your assets to appreciate tax-free for longer.

The Power of Compound Interest: How to Make Your Money Grow Over Time

Imagine your hard-earned money could grow more money! Isn't it everyone's dream? Well, it's not only a dream; it can be your reality if you harness the superpower of compound interest through your investments. Basically, compound interest is where not only your initial investment can generate returns but also the interest that's already piled up. Imagine your money growing bigger and bigger like a snowball rolling downhill. Once you've built momentum through your regular contributions toward your investment, compound interest makes your money work for you in the long run.

Then, how does compound interest differ from simple interest? In essence, compound interest grows exponentially, whereas simple interest progresses linearly. With compound interest, the bank takes into account both the original principal and the interest that has already been accumulated, but with simple interest, they just compute the initial principal. Let's examine a $1,000 savings with an annual interest rate of 5% to see how much of an interest difference there is between simple and compound interest. With simple interest, you may earn $50 in interest annually. After 10 years, your funds would reach $1,500 ($1,000 for the original funds plus $500 for interest). When compound interest is used, the interest is computed annually using the principal that has already been earned. After 10 years, the total amount will be around $1,628.

The key to maximizing the power of compound interest in your investment is through giving it time. Think of time as the magic wand that makes compound interest truly magical. Whether you're a seasoned investor or just getting started, understanding the role of time in compounding can determine whether you end up with a modest nest egg or a luxurious retirement villa in the tropics. The longer your money stays put, the more powerful compound interest becomes. Even small contributions made early can balloon into significant sums over time.

Imagine two friends, Emma and Alex, both eager to start investing for their future. Emma decides to kick things off at the ripe old age of 25, while Alex procrastinates until he hits 35. Emma puts only $200 into her investment account every month, while Alex, who starts late, decides to put $300 to make up for lost time, with both earning a 7% annual return on their investments. Now let's fast forward to when both of them are 65—meaning Emma had been consistently saving for 40 years while Alex had just 30 years. How much does Emma have? Brace yourself because Emma's nest egg would have grown to a whopping $574,648.73! That's right—over half a million dollars, thanks to the magic of compound interest. Meanwhile, Alex has only $367,647.80 at the same age. That's a significant chunk of change, no doubt, but compared to Emma, who started saving earlier with less money per month, Alex falls short by over $200,000!

So, what's the moral of the story here? Time is indeed money when it comes to compound interest. Despite Emma investing less money than Alex over 10 years apart, Emma ends up with a significantly larger nest egg than Alex. Why? Because she had time on her side. Thanks to the power of compounding, Emma's investments had more time to grow and snowball. Starting early and letting your money marinate in the market can lead to some awe-inspiring results down the line. But wait, it gets even better. Not only does starting early give your money more time to grow, but it also allows you to weather the ups and downs of the market with ease. Think of it like planting a tree—the earlier you plant it, the deeper its roots can grow, providing stability and resilience against whatever storms may come. Thinking about investing early means you're investing time, and that's the most precious commodity that even money can't buy. But hey, even if you're a bit late and haven't started, it's never too late to jump on the compound interest bandwagon. Every dollar you invest today has the potential to grow into so much more tomorrow—and that's a financial fairy tale worth believing in.

Apart from starting your investment early, building wealth through compound interest in investments means you should reinvest your dividends and interest. It's like giving your money a turbo boost on the compound interest highway. Instead of pocketing that cash from dividends and interest and calling it a day, reinvesting those earnings back into your investments can work wonders over time. Why? Because when you reinvest, you're essentially putting those dividends and interest to work for you, compounding your returns even further. Indeed, nothing is wrong about pocketing that cash and treating yourself to a fancy dinner, but can you afford to lose the opportunity to make it bigger? Think about when you reinvest those earnings back into your investment portfolio, and then the cycle repeats, accelerating your wealth accumulation and even accelerating your retirement. So, next time those dividends hit your account, think twice before splurging!

Navigating the Stock Market: Basic Strategies for Beginners

Previously, we briefly discussed how stocks allow you to have a portion of ownership of a company. So, let's now talk about where those stocks are bought and sold, known as trading activity. Imagine the bustling stock market as this vibrant marketplace where your favorite tech company or beloved pizza place publicly sells tiny pieces of their companies, and you can buy them. But why do these companies sell shares of their ownership? Well, of course, companies need money to grow and expand their business. So, instead of borrowing money from a bank, they offer ownership shares to the public through the stock market. When you buy these shares, you're essentially lending companies your money. In turn, you get dividends and capital gains.

Imagine you bought shares of a company at $10 each, and over time, the company does really well. Consequently, more people want to buy those shares, so their price goes up to $15 each. Later, if you decide to sell your shares at $15 each, you've just made **a capital gain** of $5 per share. Now, let's talk about those sweet **dividends**. When a company makes a profit, it might decide to share some of that profit with you, its shareholders. So, if you own shares in a dividend-paying company, you'll get a little slice of that profit pie regularly. It's like getting a tasty bonus just for being a shareholder.

Of course, we all want to score big with dividends and capital gains when investing our hard-earned money. But here's the thing: many of us don't take the time to research stocks thoroughly. And that can leave us feeling pretty anxious when stock prices take a dip or, worst-case scenario, we end up losing all our invested money. Yikes! So, how do you prevent those nail-biting moments? Again and again, knowledge is power. Take this subchapter as a guide to learn about investing from the basics and beyond. First and foremost, do some research before diving in. It's not only about the share price; you should focus on the underlying fundamentals of the companies you're interested in. Sure, all those financial terms might seem intimidating, but trust me, it's way easier than giving up your money when stock prices fall.

Start small with your research by surfing through financial websites and news. They'll give you the lowdown on a company's financials, track record, and even what the experts say. Plus, don't forget to pay attention to what's happening in the world around you, including economic trends, industry developments, and even global events, which can all impact the stock market. Remember, a little digging can go a long way! By understanding the company's health and future prospects, you'll feel way more confident about your choices. Plus, researching helps you avoid those one-hit-wonders and FOMO feelings when it comes to investing your money.

Apart from conducting thorough research, ensuring that you have a diversified portfolio is a must for further reducing your investment risk. Have you heard of the saying, "Don't put all your eggs in one basket?" Well, it's the golden rule of investing. Imagine you have a basket full of beautiful, fragile eggs. You wouldn't want to juggle them all at once, right? What if you dropped the basket? A slip could easily break all your eggs at once unless you spread your eggs across a few different baskets. So, make sure all your investment funds don't go into a single stock by spreading your investments across various stocks or even a mix of different investment vehicles. If you mix them strategically, you can avoid that one rotten egg spoiling the whole bunch, or even if one isn't doing well, the others might still be thriving. Sure, you might feel the impact, but because your investments are spread out, you're not putting all your investments in one risky basket.

Plus, having a diversified portfolio optimizes returns earned on your investments. You're not just putting all your hopes on that one fashion company you've always loved but also on a tech company or consumer staples company. This way, you have a better chance to benefit from different market trends.

To start diversifying your stock portfolio, invest in a few different stocks rather than putting all your money into just one, spreading out your risk right from the get-go. If you're starting to invest in stocks, opt for investing in large-cap companies first. They are already big and established, with a history of stable performance, typically having a broad customer base, diversified revenue streams, and global operations such as Amazon.com Inc. (AMZN), Microsoft Corporation (MSFT), and Apple Inc. (AAPL). Once you've got the hang of investing in large-cap companies, consider spreading your investment to mid-cap and small companies, as they may have the potential to expand rapidly, thereby increasing the value of their stock. Also, look for stocks in various industries or sectors such as technology, healthcare, finance, and consumer goods companies. That way, if one sector or industry takes a hit, the others may still perform well or even thrive.

Cryptocurrency: A Young Adult's Guide to Understanding and Investing

Imagine cash, but instead of carrying crumpled bills in your wallet, it's all digital and super secure! That's cryptocurrency, also known as crypto. It's basically digital money that lives entirely online. Unlike conventional currencies controlled by governments and banks, cryptocurrencies are decentralized. That means there's no big authority figure like a bank or government. Without the need for any intermediaries, everyone everywhere can take part in financial markets and make transactions.

So, how does it all work? Well, it's all managed by a blockchain—think of it like a super secure, transparent, and constantly updated digital ledger that keeps track of all transactions. And with the blockchain stored decentrally, it's nearly impossible for a hacker to access the entire chain in one go, ensuring that any information stored within it is as secure as Fort Knox. Since cryptocurrencies aren't linked to any specific economy or currency, their value is determined by global demand rather than national inflation. So, who knows, maybe one day you'll buy your favorite pizza with Bitcoin or send money to your friend across the globe in seconds!

Now, there is a lot of glitter surrounding cryptocurrencies, but are they all gold and rainbows? Of course, for the skyrocketing potential returns they bring, they also come with high risk. Unlike traditional investments like stocks, bonds, or real estate, cryptocurrencies take some getting used to, especially if you're not a digital native. Plus, attempting to invest in something you don't fully comprehend is a risk in itself. And while the price of cryptocurrencies can shoot up to dizzying heights, they can also swing wildly just as quickly. It's not for the faint of heart, that's for sure. So, if you're looking for stable returns, investing in cryptocurrencies might not be the best idea. Unlike stocks, where you can predict value fluctuations based on a company's track record, the cryptocurrency market fundamentally thrives on speculation. Thus, even though cryptocurrencies have been buzzing lately and gaining more and more popularity, remember they've only been around for just over a decade. It takes guts to dive into these uncharted waters as an investor, especially for beginners.

So, when you dip your toes into cryptocurrencies, approach it cautiously and only invest what you can afford to lose. To get started, you'll need to choose a cryptocurrency exchange platform where buyers and sellers meet to trade. There are many options out there, so do your research and pick one that's reputable and easy to use. Coinbase, Binance, and Kraken are some popular platforms to consider. Then, it's time to create your account—mostly just throwing in some details and verifying your identity to prevent fraud. Until the verification process is completed, you may not be able to buy or sell cryptocurrency. Depending on the platform, you may be asked to provide a copy of your passport or driver's license or even upload a selfie to verify your identity. Once your account is verified, you'll need to deposit funds into your crypto account by linking your bank account or making a payment with a debit or credit card. Depending on the exchange, there may be a waiting period before you can access your deposited funds. With your wallet loaded, it's time to go cryptocurrency shopping. Whether you're eyeing Bitcoin, Ethereum, Dogecoin, or the latest hype coin, just click "buy," enter your desired amount and boom—you're officially part of the crypto market!

Now that you own some crypto, you need to store it safely. You wouldn't just leave cash lying around, would you?

Immediately after buying cryptocurrency, it's typically stored in a so-called crypto wallet within your exchange account. They're convenient for quick transactions but might not be the most secure option for long-term storage. So, opt for either hot or cold wallets. If you prefer a convenient and easily accessible option that operates online and on internet-connected devices, hot wallets are the way to go, despite the increased risk of theft due to their internet connection. On the other hand, cold wallets remain offline by default, providing maximum security for your crypto assets. Cold wallets typically come in the form of external devices such as USB or hard drives. But remember, if you lose the key code associated with them or the device breaks or fails, access to that cryptocurrency may be lost for good.

FIVE

Digital Literacy and Security

In today's digital age, understanding digital literacy and security isn't just about keeping up with the latest social media trends—it's an absolute necessity for navigating the online world safely. As we're constantly sharing our lives, thoughts, and experiences online, it comes with inherent risks, from getting scammed and experiencing data breaches to falling victim to malware infections, phishing attacks, and even identity theft. These threats not only damage your reputation and credibility but could also lead to blackmail, financial loss, and even emotional distress. That's why learning about digital literacy equips us with the knowledge to protect ourselves in the vast landscape of the internet and make informed decisions about what we share online. It's about empowering ourselves to navigate the digital realm with confidence, awareness, and resilience.

Crafting Your Digital Identity: Managing Your Online Presence

In today's digital age, where everyone is constantly online, building a positive online image isn't just an option—it's a necessity, not only for businesses but also for individuals like us. Your online presence is more than just a fun social media thing like those cute selfies or hilarious memes you post; it reflects who you are and what you represent. Being aware of your online presence means defining yourself, your skills, and your values in a way that distinguishes you from others, ultimately shaping how others perceive you. Your digital footprint isn't only visible to your friends and family but also to your colleagues, future employers, and even that cute person you follow on social media. Crazy, right, that your online presence affects your entire life? Imagine your online presence like leaving behind a trail of breadcrumbs that literally anyone can follow. Indeed, it is wild how your online image can affect your life. But don't freak out! Maintaining a positive online image isn't rocket science. It starts with being mindful of what you post, comment, and share on your social media. On a side note, make sure your online profiles show off your awesome personality, share your passions, and spread positivity.

However, remember that putting yourself out there online means everyone can see your profile, which also means you need to be aware of your own privacy. Of course, no one wants their information to be used by malicious individuals for spamming, identity theft, or other harmful purposes. So, set your privacy settings to keep your personal info safe from prying eyes. And hey, most importantly, think twice before sharing sensitive stuff like your phone number, home address, email address, any financial transactions, passwords, and personal details like social security number, passport information, or any other government-issued identification numbers. Remember, once you share something on social media, it can be difficult to control who sees it or how it's used.

Alongside the positive aspects of connecting with others, showcasing your talents, and sharing your passions through online platforms, it also means you'll inevitably deal with digital negativity and cyberbullying around the corner. But here's the thing: you get to control the vibe of your online platform. So, as positivity attracts positivity, share only things that make you happy, inspire others, and spread good cheer to attract more of the same. And when someone throws a silly insult your way, just laugh it off. Remind yourself that it's more a reflection of who they are rather than who you are. If someone is being nasty, don't waste your energy trying to enlighten them; just block them and move on. Most importantly, focus more on the ones that constantly support you to help you drown out the negativity.

Cybersecurity Basics: Protecting Yourself Online

Every day, we browse websites, access emails, and surf social media for both pleasure and necessity without even realizing we're exposing ourselves to dangers. You know those emails that pop into your inbox promising you've won a million bucks, getting a job offer without an interview, or claiming to be from a long-lost relative in a far-off land? Yeah, those are the dangers we're talking about. Once you find yourself clicking those links or downloading something, the next thing you know, all your personal information is in their hands. So, to start being cautious and aware of how to spot them, ask yourself, "Does it sound too good to be true?" If yes, it probably is. Also, if they create a sense of urgency to rush you into making a decision, whether to click the link or download anything, take a step back so you can think clearly. That's when you double-check the sender's email address or the URL they're directing you to. Sometimes, it'll be a dead giveaway that something's not right. Plus, if they ever ask you to provide sensitive information like passwords or credit card numbers via email, it is definitely a scam.

Now that you know how to spot a scam, it's time to build a fort around your online accounts by creating strong, unique passwords. Do you still use your pet's name, your girlfriend's or boyfriend's name, or worse, the classic one, your birthday? Or is your password all the same for every site you sign up for? If yes, you may likely be targeted right now by scammers out there. Think about it: Weak passwords are like leaving your doors wide open for hackers to stroll right in and help themselves to your personal information, bank accounts, or embarrassing old photos. So, start to change your old passwords to be a sweet spot between easy-to-recall and difficult-to-guess. Also, make sure you use different passwords on different sites to make it even safer and prevent scammers from trying to use stolen credentials on other sites. However, using different passwords for different sites also comes with the need to remember them, which, let's be honest, is nearly impossible. But fear not; you can use a password manager that is locked with one master password. Password managers save your passwords for each account and store them in an encrypted vault so you don't have to memorize them all. So next time you're on your laptop, phone, or tablet, no more scrambling to find that note with your login details because now you have your password manager that can sync seamlessly across all devices.

Another security measure necessary is keeping your device's software up to date. Think of software as a fortress protecting your precious data from digital invaders, so you need regular upkeep to stay impenetrable. That means regularly updating your software to fend off hacks and malware. By promptly installing updates, you close unsecured loopholes, as updates often include patches for hackers' vulnerabilities. Also, software updates often come equipped with enhanced security features designed to detect and block the latest malware threats. So next time you see your software needs an update, don't click the "later" button; update it right away.

Other than having strong passwords stored in a safe password manager and keeping the software updated, protecting yourself online means ensuring that every online financial transaction you make is secure. When making transactions, always look for the "https://" in the website address, as the "s" stands for secure, indicating your connection is encrypted and protected. Most importantly, avoid conducting financial transactions over public Wi-Fi networks in your favorite coffee shop or at the airport while waiting for boarding, as they may be susceptible to interception by hackers. Consider waiting for a more secure network to handle those important transactions. Plus, use a virtual private network (VPN) for an added layer of encryption, especially if you travel a lot and need to make transactions anywhere.

The Influence of Social Media: Use and Abuse in the Modern Age

As of 2024, over 5.04 billion people, which makes up over 62% of the world's population, are social media users (Petrosyan, 2024). No wonder social media and its buzz are becoming more and more influential these days. Social media isn't merely a platform for sharing, liking, commenting, and uploading hilarious posts; it's much more than that. It amplifies voices, connects people across continents, and shapes the way we communicate. Thus, social media has become a powerful force to spark social movements and even political revolutions. So why not leverage social media for your own benefit? Think of your social media profiles as your personal brand—it's all about showcasing the best version of you!

But before you start auditing your online profiles, know your social media goals. Whether it's building a personal brand, growing your network, creating meaningful connections, showcasing creativity, promoting personal growth, spreading positivity, or even educating and informing your audience, you can do anything with your online profiles. However, choose a goal that aligns with your values, passions, and overall vision of your online presence. When you've nailed down your goals, choose the social media platform where you can shine the brightest, whether it's LinkedIn for professional networking, Instagram for visual storytelling, or Twitter for sharing quick updates and insights. Then, it's time to start posting about yourself but remember, always be true when sharing your story, journey, and even your failures. And remember, only share stuff that reflects your passions and interests. After all, you're building a personal brand, so showcase the content you're truly proud of!

However, building a personal brand entails more than just broadcasting your message; it also involves cultivating relationships and actively engaging with your audience. So, make time to respond to comments, join conversations, and show genuine interest in others. Most importantly, consistency is key to building a unique personal brand, whether posting regular updates, maintaining a cohesive visual style, or staying true to your brand voice.

Aside from bringing people worldwide closer together, social media also comes with its downsides. How many times have you scrolled through your feed and felt everyone else has their life together except you? Seeing your friends post about their epic adventures often makes you feel you're missing out on all the fun. And don't even get me started on the addiction factor. Check your phone; how many hours have you been on social media? It's so easy to get sucked into endless scrolling, chasing those likes and notifications like they're the key to happiness. So, whenever your mind spirals into these feelings, know that every video, photo, and post you see online isn't always the whole picture. Consider setting boundaries, taking regular breaks, and prioritizing real-life relationships to help promote a healthier relationship with social media.

Although social media has become a big part of our lives, be aware that it may often include fake news and misinformation. So, just because something is trending or has thousands of shares doesn't automatically make it true. Take a moment to pause and ask yourself: Where did this information come from? Is the source reliable? What evidence supports it? Then, do your own fact-check by seeing if other credible sources report the same information or verify with fact-checking websites like *Snopes*, *FactCheck.org*, or *PolitiFact*. So, keep being skeptical about accepting online information, especially from social media.

Digital Footprints: Understanding and Managing Your Online History

Think about walking on a sandy beach. With every step, you leave an imprint where you've been. Your digital footprint is kind of like that, but instead of being washed away by the waves, its traces hardly can be washed away, showing the trail of data you leave behind as you interact with the internet. Whenever you browse a website, post on social media, or shop online, you create a digital footprint. It's a collection of data that shows what you've done online, and it can stick around for a long time, sometimes even forever. This means that mistakes or indiscretions made online can come back to haunt you years down the line, affecting your future prospects and relationships.

Even though right now, as you read this paragraph, the idea of an exposed digital footprint seems harmless, be aware that your digital footprint contains a wealth of personal information, more than you can imagine, from your browsing history and social media posts to your online purchases and location data. Not only can this information be tracked, collected, and analyzed by companies or advertisers, but hackers and scammers may compromise your privacy, leading to identity theft or cyberattacks.

Knowing that what you post defines not only who you were in the past but also who you are today should make you more mindful of what you share online. Whenever you want to post anything, ask yourself whether it is really appropriate to share online. Then, it's time to check out those old posts and pics. Ask yourself, "Do they still represent the person I am today?" If not, it might be time for a little clean-up session.

Aside from auditing your own social media profiles, you should start to search your name on Google, as it might be the very first thing your potential employer, coworker, or even potential romantic partner sees. When you search for your name on Google, look closely at what comes up on the first few pages of search results. If you come across any inappropriate or concerning information related to your name that potentially harms your reputation, don't hesitate to reach out to the website owner to update the content or remove it entirely. Remember to provide any relevant information or documentation to support your case.

Email Etiquette: Communicating Professionally in the Digital World

Being digitally literate goes way beyond just mastering social media. Indeed, social media is a big part of our online lives, but email is a fundamental tool for professional communication, and using it effectively requires proper etiquette. Think about knowing email etiquette as being as important as having a flawless first impression with a firm handshake, neat attire, and warm gestures—it sets the tone for respectful and professional settings. So, let's get through the key details your email should include. Subject lines are the first thing your email recipient sees, so ensure it concisely summarizes the email's content. Then, include a polite and appropriate greeting after the subject line. After greetings, state the purpose of your email in the opening paragraph. Use clear and concise language to convey your message, and organize your content into paragraphs for readability. When you're done with the body part of the email, end your email with a courteous closing such as "Thank you," "Sincerely," or "Best regards," followed by your name or any relevant contact information if needed.

To keep your email game sharp, dodge some all-too-common pitfalls, starting with ditching all slang you constantly use in your personal chatroom. Slang won't jazz your email up; instead, using polished professional language will show more professionalism. Although you're emailing your close coworker who you know well, keep the tone professional, preventing being overly casual. It's all about striking that perfect balance between friendly and professional. And don't forget the dreaded reply-all button, which is essentially and mostly a recipe for disaster. We've all been there accidentally hitting "reply all" when only one person needed the info. So, before you unleash chaos in your inbox, take a moment to pause and consider who really needs to see your response.

Not only being aware of email etiquette but also managing your email inbox is crucial as it significantly affects your productivity at work. Start with using folders and filters for all your emails in the inbox with "Important," "To-Do," or "Projects" labels to help keep your inbox clutter-free and find things quickly. Further, set specific times to check emails because many people get obsessed with being on time, making them constantly check emails throughout the day. Instead, consider setting aside specific time to check and respond to emails to minimize distractions. Other than being effective and productive regarding work email, again and again, ensure your email security by not sharing sensitive information in emails. Avoid opening attachments or clicking links from unknown senders, as they might contain malware or lead to cyberattacks on your work email.

SIX

Mental Health Matters

We juggle a lot—studies, jobs, social lives—and it's easy to let stress take hold. Ever feel like you're running on fumes, overwhelmed by the pressures of life but unsure how to stop the cycle? You're not alone. Mental health struggles are widespread, especially among young adults. Even though it's entirely common, we can't underestimate its power to weigh us down. So, let's engrave it in our minds that our mental health matters. Prioritizing mental health isn't just a luxury; it's an investment in our overall well-being, which is much more important than maintaining physical health. It all starts with knowing the real importance of getting enough sleep, managing everyday stress, navigating depression, being mindful, and building resilience within ourselves.

Recognizing and Managing Stress: Techniques That Work

People often assume that the transition from older teens to adulthood is a carefree time, full of fun and adventure, with no stress in sight. After all, what could be so difficult about being young, right? However, the reality is far from this misconception. Over the course of the academic year, youths reported higher levels of stress than the average adult recorded. Adults reported an average stress level of only 5.1, compared to 5.8 for youths (Bethune, 2014). The fact that younger people are more stressed than adults shouldn't be taken lightly. What's even more troubling is that younger people don't seem to realize how much stress may actually affect their physical and mental health. You might wonder why stress levels are higher among younger individuals like you. Well, transitions happen a lot at your age, making stress seem to be around every corner—whether it's looming deadlines at work, pressure to excel in your career, changes in your own body, having too high expectations of yourself, or the never-ending quest to figure out what you want to do with your life. The worst part is that, compared to adults, you have little to no resources to cope with the feelings inside you.

So, to help build those stress management resources within you, know your own stress triggers first. Observe your body's response to different circumstances. Do you get sweaty palms before meeting new people or having to present your slides? Or do you get tight shoulders during a hectic routine?

Sometimes, it's not only the situation triggering you to experience these physical signs, but how you think about it may affect you more. So, ask yourself, "What am I worried or scared about?" When you know what your common stress patterns look like to you, start developing your own coping mechanisms to keep your cool and manage stress in a healthy way. Practicing deep breathing can be a game-changer as it only takes seconds to practice, but it effectively helps you quiet the chaos swirling in your mind and bring a sense of calm. Or, when life starts to feel like too much, set some time aside, whether it's the very first thing you do in the morning or the last thing at night, for five to ten minutes to meditate. Sitting quietly and letting go of your racing thoughts allows you to recharge and find clarity amidst the chaos. And let's not forget the power of physical activity—it can be your best friend. Going for a run or hitting the gym isn't just about staying in shape; it's also a fantastic way to release built-up tension and boost those feel-good endorphins. Most importantly, only you can find what works best for you, so don't be afraid to take some trial and error until you find what resonates with you. And remember, it's okay to ask for help if you need it. Whether it's talking to parents or friends, seeking guidance from a therapist, or joining a support group, there's strength in reaching out and leaning on others during tough times.

Navigating Anxiety and Depression: Understanding and Finding Help

We all encounter stress now and then, but sometimes, it can morph into something bigger. Even though everyone may encounter similar daily stressors every day from work, college, or personal life, everyone experiences stress differently. For some, it might be that constant tension in their shoulders, while for others, it can manifest as racing thoughts and an inability to relax. When you find stress starting to affect your daily life and functioning, it might be a sign that something more serious is going on. That's why it's fundamental to recognize the warning signs. Anxiety itself can show in a wide range of ways, from constant worry and restlessness to panic attacks and physical symptoms like sweating or trembling. On the other hand, depression might often present as persistent sadness, loss of interest in things once enjoyed, changes in sleep patterns or appetite, and even thoughts of self-harm or, worse, suicide. Sometimes, in the early phase of anxiety and depression, we might brush off these symptoms, thinking they'll go away on their own, when, in fact, those signs of anxiety and depression won't just disappear on their own. To get you back on track, identifying its early signs is not enough; you need to take conscious steps to make them go away for good. First, make self-care a priority by setting aside time for enjoyable and relaxing activities. Whether it's going for a stroll in the outdoors, engaging in mindfulness or meditation, or spending time on an activity you are fond of, schedule time for these activities on a regular basis. Whenever feeling like a failure haunts you, embrace the power of "yet." Instead of screaming, "I can't do this," replace it with "I can't do this *yet*" to acknowledge the struggle while keeping the door open for future success. Then, train your brain to ditch negativity bias and challenge them with more positive ones.

Even though these self-help strategies may make a world of difference, there are cases when you may want a bit more help if your issue becomes more serious, such as interfering with your daily life and lasting weeks or months or even when you are considering self-harm or suicide. However, remember that seeking help does not mean you are losing the battle; instead, it is a sign of strength to find a partner in navigating these murky waters. So, start talking to your primary care provider, as they can offer advice and even connect you with therapists who can help. Indeed, the idea of getting therapy might sound intimidating, but think about it as just a safe space to talk about what's on your mind and get the support you most need to start feeling better. And if you're worried about the cost, don't sweat it—there are often options for reduced fees or sliding scale payments, especially at community mental health centers.

Alongside seeking therapy and counseling, consider the possibility of medication if recommended by your healthcare provider. However, medication is a personal decision, so there is no pressure to take it if you're not comfortable yet. So, ask about potential side effects, how long it takes for the medication to work, and anything else on your mind before starting the medication. Be open about any concerns you have about medication, such as potential dependence or interactions with other medications you're taking.

The Importance of Sleep: Strategies for a Better Night's Rest

Balancing school and work while trying your hardest to squeeze in some personal time is indeed one of the toughest challenges of transitioning to adulthood. Amidst this chaos, sleep often takes a back seat, making getting enough sleep on a regular basis seem like a dream. As much as people emphasize the importance of exercise and a healthy diet, sleep is equally vital to support healthy brain function and maintain overall physical health. Have you ever heard of our body's incredible internal clock called the circadian rhythm? It's like having a clock inside of us that regulates when we feel sleepy and when we feel awake. This rhythm is influenced by various factors such as light exposure, eating habits, and even our daily routines. Think about it: When darkness falls, our body starts winding down, producing melatonin that makes us feel drowsy and cozy, while sunlight streaming through our window tells our body, "Alright, time to wake up and seize the day."

Now, the problem with our crazy-busy lives is that we often mess with this natural rhythm. We pull all-nighters cramming for exams, work late shifts that bleed into the morning, and then maybe catch some shut-eye when the sun's already up. This throws our internal clock way off balance. That's why you often wake up feeling groggy and irritable, while at night, you're tossing and turning in bed. And it doesn't end there. Not getting enough sleep can lead to a whole host of other mental health issues, from increased stress and difficulty concentrating to even depression. Plus, the lack of sleep can weaken our immune system, making us more susceptible to illness. It's like we're running on empty, trying to function without giving our bodies the necessary fuel.

Improving your sleep isn't as complicated as rocket science; creating a sleep-friendly environment is totally doable for everyone. With a few tweaks here and there, you can transform your bedroom into a haven for quality rest. Quality sleep is not just about how many hours you spend hitting the pillow; there are other factors contributing to our overall restfulness. First, ensure your bedroom is as dark as possible when ready to hit the hay. To block out streetlights and early morning sunlight, think about purchasing shades or blackout drapes. But, when you're awake, expose yourself to natural light during the day to help control your circadian rhythm. Next, choose comfortable bedding and a blanket, and keep your room comfortably cool. Plus, minimize disruptive noise by using earplugs if it's disturbing your sleep or playing soothing sounds if complete silence during sleep isn't your thing. Not only creating a sleep-friendly environment but also letting your body wind down about 15 to 30 minutes before bed can be a great idea. At this time, limit your screen usage since blue light from screens can interrupt your body's circadian cycle. Instead, take up soothing hobbies like reading or having a warm bath. Also, aim to maintain a consistent sleep schedule by going to bed and waking up at roughly the same time every day, including weekends.

If you still find yourself struggling to fall asleep despite creating a conducive environment, it might be insomnia. So, try practicing deep breathing or meditation for a few minutes before bed. If sleep issues persist despite your efforts, don't hesitate to seek professional guidance from a healthcare provider or sleep specialist. Alternatively, if you're struggling to fall asleep due to a condition involving pauses in breathing during sleep accompanied by loud snoring or gasping for air, called sleep apnea, consider seeking medical advice as you may need to make some lifestyle changes or use CPAP machines.

The Power of Mindfulness: Practices for Mental Well-Being

As life can get pretty hectic with all the stuff we've got going on and stress hitting us like a bus, we need to prioritize our mental well-being by practicing mindfulness. Mindfulness isn't just some trendy buzzword; it's our ticket to navigating through the craziness with a little more grace and much less overwhelming. While juggling a million things at once can easily become overwhelming, practicing mindfulness can lead to less overthinking, reduced stress levels, sharper memory, laser-focused attention, and a calmer response to life's curveballs (Davis & Hayes, 2012). Whether you're diving into formal meditation sessions, seeking counseling with a mindfulness-based therapist, or just sneaking in a few minutes of mindfulness during your daily grind, being mindful brings those wide-ranging benefits to you.

But don't worry, to start practicing mindfulness, you don't need to burn incense or sit in perfect posture for hours. When practicing mindfulness, the key is to attain a state of alertness while concentrating on relaxation by paying attention to thoughts and sensations without passing judgment. So, start with something you can do for a few minutes, which you can easily squeeze into your daily routine. First off, begin with breathing exercises with closed eyes while focusing on your breath. With every breath in and breath out, feel your belly rise and fall. Bring your focus back to your breathing if you notice your attention has wandered. Or, whether you're chowing down on your favorite snack or just chilling out, practice being mindful by savoring the experience. Notice the colors, textures, and smells of your food. To make this a daily habit, slowly start incorporating these practices by focusing on present sensations during everyday activities. At first, these mindful practices may not seem relaxing at all, but over time, they surely improve your self-awareness as you become comfortable with other, more involved practices.

Building Resilience: Overcoming Challenges and Setbacks

As we all know, life throws curveballs when we least expect it, and no matter how hard we try to dodge them, they still find a way to hit us. But what if, instead of getting knocked down every time, you could bounce back stronger? That's the power of resilience—the ability to handle whatever comes your way. Feeling stressed about your upcoming project presentation at work? Resilience helps you develop healthy coping mechanisms to deal with pressure and challenges, preventing stress from eating you alive. Feeling down after not receiving a single interview invitation despite months of trying? With resilience, you learn to pick yourself up, dust yourself off, and keep moving forward, no longer getting stuck in your own negative self-talk. Tough times may happen now and then, which feels painful at times, but they don't have to define who you are or what you'll be in the future. You have the control to shape your own life and grow from them.

So, how do you become more resilient? Like building muscle, increasing your resilience in the face of adversity takes time and requires you to be intentional during tough times. It all starts with having a positive outlook on life in every situation, especially the hard times. With each small victory in your life, remind yourself that you can achieve them due to your own ability to overcome obstacles. Instead of resisting change within your progress, try to embrace it as an opportunity to learn and grow to be more adaptable. Plus, setting realistic goals for yourself is essential—setting unrealistic goals only sets you up for disaster, making failing to achieve goals daunting. So, choose to set more achievable goals that build confidence and keep you motivated, which is vital for resilience.

However, as life can get increasingly overwhelming, asking for help won't hurt, especially if you've been constantly down, daily tasks feel impossible, and you're struggling to cope with negative thoughts. Talking things out with someone you trust can be a huge weight off your shoulders, knowing that they can provide you with support and guidance to get through the problems. Or, in cases where support from friends and family might not be enough, seek support from mental health professionals who can provide more practical strategies to help you cope with mental health issues. Remember, you're not alone, and asking for help is a courageous step toward healing and growth.

SEVEN

Health and Wellbeing

Amidst the chaos of our daily routines and responsibilities, taking care of ourselves is a non-negotiable necessity for living a fulfilling and vibrant life. Most importantly, it's about keeping our bodies in motion. While we may feel invincible and perfectly in tune with ourselves, unexpected bumps in the road, like illnesses or accidents, can happen to anyone. That's why prioritizing our health remains a priority—not only ensuring that you're healthy now but also building healthy habits for the future. From exercising regularly to scheduling routine health check-ups, let's make this journey towards healthier wellbeing our personal quest. And let's not forget the importance of having health insurance—a safety net that ensures access to quality care when we need it most. So, let's commit to being our healthiest selves, where self-care isn't an indulgence but a sacred commitment to honoring the incredible gift of life itself.

Exercise for Everyone: Finding What Works for You

Between classes, the never-ending to-do list, work deadlines, and late-night social sprints, it's easy to feel like a drained battery by the end, or even the middle, of the week. You know that feeling when even that third cup of coffee can't quite jolt you awake? Well, what if I told you there's a more effective way to boost your energy levels? Enter exercise.

Exercise isn't just about getting those gains or fitting into that favorite pair of jeans (though those are great perks, too). Regular exercise boosts your energy levels naturally without making your heart race like that third cup of coffee. It might seem counterintuitive—how spending a whole lot of energy through exercising can increase your energy levels. But as you exercise, it boosts your circulation, gets oxygen flowing to your brain, and revs up your metabolism, leaving you feeling more alert, focused, and ready to take on the world. No more mid-afternoon energy crashes during work or dragging yourself through lectures.

And here's the kicker: Exercise not only enhances physical health but also improves mental well-being by reducing anxiety, depression, and negative moods, as well as boosting self-esteem and cognitive function (Sharma et al., 2006). Ever notice how you feel like you're on top of the world after a good workout? That's because exercise releases endorphins, those feel-good chemicals in your brain that lift your spirits and chase away those pesky blues. The best part is that exercising isn't just about those immediate effects; it's also about the long-term benefits, as it lowers your risk of chronic diseases while strengthening your muscles and bones. So, not only will you look and feel great now, but you'll also be setting yourself up for a healthier, happier future.

But wait, it gets even better. You don't need to spend hours at the gym to reap those benefits. Even short bursts of activity can make a big difference. So start exercising today by taking the stairs instead of the elevator, taking a brief walk to the park with your dog, or trying a fun dance workout video in your room. However, don't start with making exercise as one of the chores. When exercise feels more like a chore, you're less likely to stick with it. So, choosing the exercises you enjoy most is the key to making exercise a sustainable habit.

Be bold and explore different types of physical activity until you find something that clicks. Whether it's jogging, yoga, swimming, dancing, or kickboxing, there's a whole world of options out there. To start exploring what exercise you enjoy, consider your interests and preferences. Do you love being outdoors? Maybe hiking or cycling would be a good fit. Are you a social butterfly? Group fitness classes or team sports could be right up your alley. Keep an open mind and be willing to step out of your comfort zone—you might just discover a new passion! While exploring various exercise options, start listening to your body to decide which one leaves you feeling energized and invigorated or drained and bored.

When it comes to starting regular exercise, finding a sweet spot between ambitious and realistic goals is key to staying motivated and focused; instead of setting vague goals like "get fit" or "lose weight," be specific about what you want to achieve and make it quantifiable, whether it's tracking the number of pounds you lift, the distance you run, or the inches you lose. While it's great to aim high, ensure your goals are attainable, given your current fitness level, schedule, and resources. Keep in mind that setting unrealistic goals only leads to frustration and burnout. Most importantly, you need to be consistent instead of pushing yourself to the limit in every workout. Instead, slow and steady progress is more sustainable than trying to make dramatic changes overnight.

Despite our best intentions, a whole lot of barriers often get in the way of regular exercise. But you need to be disciplined with yourself. Don't have the time to exercise? Make sure you block off dedicated time for exercise, whether first thing in the morning, during lunch break, or after work, and treat that time like any other important appointment in your day. Long exercises make you bored? Break it into shorter sessions throughout the day, aiming for ten to fifteen minutes at a time—they add up. Not motivated even to start exercising? When you've found an activity you actually enjoy, grab a friend, join a workout class, or put on your favorite music to make it fun.

The Importance of Routine Health Check-Ups

"I am young, nothing can hurt me" or "I don't have health concerns in my body" are probably the first thoughts that come to your mind when talking about health check-ups. As you're feeling completely fine right now, it's easy to brush off regular visits to the doctor. But who can guarantee that you might not already have some health issues waiting to become bigger ones in just another year or two? That's why being proactive by taking routine health check-ups is vital. Yeah, I know, going to the doctor's office might not be the most exciting thing on your to-do list, but trust me, it's worth it. The more you know about your body, the better equipped you are to make healthy choices. Plus, regular visits help you build a relationship with your doctor, making it easier to talk about any concerns you might have in the future.

During these visits, get ready for a quick physical exam on your heart and lungs, checking your blood pressure, and taking a peek at your ears, nose, and throat. Depending on your current health, age, and risk factors, your doctor might recommend certain screenings. They'll also talk to you about your lifestyle habits, like diet, exercise, and sleep, and offer advice on how to stay healthy. Based on your check-up, your doctor will discuss any necessary next steps, including lifestyle changes, further testing, or referrals to specialists. Remember, during the check-up, don't be afraid to ask questions and voice any concerns.

Other than a routine health check-up, ensure you have been vaccinated to prevent serious diseases such as measles, mumps, meningitis, and HPV. Getting vaccines means you are training your body to recognize and fight off germs before they can make you sick. When you get vaccinated, you protect yourself from diseases and create a protective shield around the community, making it harder for diseases to spread. Don't believe the hype about vaccination's scary side effects; some are entirely safe and have undergone thorough evaluation. Do your research if you are hesitant about taking any vaccine or medication. Or, are you reluctant to get vaccinated because people say that you can build immunity naturally through infection? It is true, but getting infected with diseases often comes with a much greater risk of severe complications or even death. It all comes down to research and what you feel comfortable taking.

Taking preventive healthcare measures does not end with routine health check-ups and getting vaccinations; finding the right healthcare provider and understanding your health insurance is sometimes the hardest part when adulting. So, it's better to get recommendations from your friends and family first. Also, consider scheduling a consultation or asking questions to ensure they're the right fit for your needs. Or, do your own check online about the healthcare provider, especially regarding who accepts your insurance. Then, the next thing you should do is understand your health insurance coverage. Indeed, it can be confusing at first, with a lot of new terms coming into your head at once, but once you know the terms and conditions around your insurance coverage, especially what your out-of-pocket costs might be, it saves you a lot of money in the future. If you're unsure about something, contact your insurance provider for clarification.

First Aid Skills Every Adult Should Know

Talking about first aid might seem like one of those things you only see on TV dramas or in boring health classes, but trust me, knowing how to handle common emergencies can be a literal lifesaver in real life. Whether it's a family member, a friend, or even a stranger, being able to step in during an emergency can make all the difference. Having basic first aid knowledge means you're prepared no matter where you are. Think of learning these basic first aid skills as being as important as learning how to cook a meal—something that everyone should know, regardless of age or background. So, below are some basic first aid steps you can learn.

- If you've got scrapes and cuts, start by cleaning the wound with cool running water and mild soap. Apply gentle pressure with a clean cloth to stop any bleeding. Once clean, cover with a bandage to keep out dirt. Monitor the injury for signs of infection, such as redness, swelling, or pus, and seek medical attention if necessary.
- For bumps and bruises, apply ice wrapped in a cloth to reduce swelling for the first 24 hours. After that, use the warmth of a heating pad to relieve any soreness. These usually heal on their own, but if there's severe pain or swelling, see a doctor.
- If someone's heart is not beating, performing CPR or using an AED can help restart the heart or recirculate blood until the heart can be started with defibrillation. If you think someone is having a cardiac arrest, assign a person nearby to call 911. Start chest compressions using both hands, pushing down hard and fast in the center of the chest. Keep going until someone with more training or a healthcare professional arrives. If accessible, use an AED (Automated External Defibrillator), which

can administer an electric shock to restore normal heart rhythm. These first aid devices are designed to be user-friendly, even for individuals with no training. First, activate the AED and follow the voice prompts. Apply the electrode pads to the person's bare chest, ensuring no one is touching the individual. Then, press the "analyze" button. If the AED recommends a shock, press the "shock" button. After administering the shock, continue CPR until assistance arrives or the person begins breathing normally.

- Signs of allergic reactions include trouble breathing, itching, swelling, hives, and nausea. Try to determine the cause of the allergic reaction, whether it's a certain food or insect sting, and remove it if possible. If the person has a known allergy and carries an EpiPen, help them administer it as instructed. If the reaction is severe, usually involving trouble breathing and wheezing, immediately call emergency services.

- If someone is choking and showing signs of not being able to speak, prompt them to cough forcefully in an attempt to dislodge the object. If coughing is ineffective, perform abdominal thrusts, also known as the Heimlich maneuver. Stand behind the person, wrap your arms around their waist, and deliver upward thrusts into the abdomen until the object is expelled.

- For burns, begin by removing the source of the burn and then cool the affected area with cool running water for at least 10 minutes if it's a minor burn that affects only the outer layer of skin, resulting in redness and swelling. Avoid popping blisters, as this can raise the risk of infection. If the burn causes blistering, redness, and swelling, is larger than three inches wide, affects sensitive areas like the face, hands, feet, genitals, or is over a major joint, call emergency services immediately. Also, refrain from removing any clothing stuck to the burn.

Now that we've learned how to perform basic first aid and respond to common medical emergencies, let's talk about how to create a well-stocked first aid kit for both home and travel. First aid kits are available in various sizes and designs and can be bought at your local drugstore. There are also kits tailored for specific activities like hiking, camping, or boating. Whether you opt for a pre-made kit or assemble one yourself, ensure it includes personal items such as medications, emergency contact numbers, or any other items recommended by your healthcare provider.

Everyday items that should be included in your first aid kit are adhesive bandages, sterile gauze pads, antiseptic wipes or solution, scissors, disposable gloves, pain relievers such as acetaminophen or ibuprofen, and antihistamines. Remember to check your kit regularly and replace any expired items. When traveling, tailor your kit to your destination and activities. Consider including insect repellent, sunscreen, and medication for motion sickness. Pack your kit in a sturdy, portable case that's easy to identify.

To take it a step further, consider taking a formal first aid course to enhance your emergency preparedness. These trainings provide you with the knowledge and skills to respond confidently and effectively in emergencies. Not only will you learn proper techniques, but this training will improve your ability to assess situations quickly and make informed decisions in high-stress environments. Who knows, you may become a true lifesaver, making the difference between life and death for someone in need.

Understanding Health Insurance: Navigating Your Options

In 2021, a whopping 27 million people in the US alone were uninsured, even after getting hit by the COVID-19 pandemic (United States Census Bureau, 2022). Let's face it: healthcare costs in the States can be as steep as a mountain hike. So, why do people still choose to go uninsured? Well, for starters, most people get health insurance through their job, but not everyone's lucky enough to have that option. Plus, even if employer-sponsored coverage is offered, some people may struggle to afford their portion of the premium. Aside from eligibility and affordability, some people simply feel they're completely healthy and don't need health insurance yet, while others find the sign-up process too confusing (Tolbert et al., 2022). But here's the fact: being uninsured does not save you money —it's actually quite the opposite. Paying for medical bills without insurance can drain your bank account faster than you can say, "ouch." Imagine having to dip into your savings or borrow money from friends just to cover a trip to the ER.

Not exactly the kind of adventure you were hoping for, right? And let's not forget the stress. About 75% of uninsured adults are constantly sweating over how they'll pay their medical bills, especially in emergencies (Tolbert et al., 2022). Do you *really* want to risk all that just to avoid paying for health insurance premiums? Sure, paying for health insurance might feel like a drag now, but trust me, the peace of mind of knowing you're covered when life throws you a curveball? Totally worth it.

So, let's do ourselves a favor and investigate a few common insurance options that you may select from. The more familiar you are with the plans available, the better prepared you'll be to pick one that suits your budget and healthcare needs.

- **Health Maintenance Organization (HMO) Plan:** This plan grants you access to a bunch of healthcare services like check-ups, primary care, and hospital visits. But, you've gotta stick to their network of chosen healthcare providers. As a preliminary step of signing up for this plan, it often requires you as the member to select a Primary Care Physician (PCP) within the network to be your go-to for all things health. Want to see a specialist? You'll need the PCP's stamp of approval first. The good news? Low premiums, minimal paperwork, minimal copays, and lower out-of-pocket costs for covered services, with the least amount of paperwork needed compared to other plans. But remember, if you stray outside the network, you'll be footing the bill except in emergencies.

- **Preferred Provider Organization (PPO) Plan:** This plan offers you more options compared to an HMO. Still, members are encouraged to visit a network of preferred healthcare services and facilities. PPOs, however, cover both in-network and out-of-network treatments; nonetheless, the cost of out-of-network services may be much more costly. Unlike HMOs, PPO members are not required to choose a PCP or obtain a PCP's referral before consulting a specialist. But beware— flexibility comes at a cost. PPOs are more likely to come with higher premiums and out-of-pocket expenses, especially if you visit an out-of-network healthcare provider often. With PPOs, you must submit a claim for reimbursement after seeing an out-of-network healthcare provider.

- **Fee-for-Service (FFS) Plan:** This plan is like having the golden ticket to healthcare freedom. You can go to any doctor you want, whenever you want. But guess what? You've gotta pay upfront for everything. Then, you file a claim with your insurance company to get reimbursement. Further, with an FFS plan, an annual deductible must be paid before the insurance provider starts to pay the costs. You only have to pay a portion of the medical bills—referred to as coinsurance—after you reach the specified deductible level; the insurance company will take care of the remaining balance. That's why FFS plans are usually the priciest

options available, with costs that can differ
significantly according to your residence, age, and
the benefits you want to add.

When comparing these plans, take a look back at the kind of medical treatment you've had in the past. Understanding your medical history can give you insight into your typical healthcare needs. Plus, you'll want to consider whether you're okay with plans that require referrals before you can see a specialist. Making the right decision when it comes to choosing which insurance plan to have hinges on how well you understand some key terms, especially about what you need to pay. First and foremost, when you have an insurance plan, you must pay a premium for your coverage, typically on a monthly basis. Think of it like your membership fee for being part of the insurance club. The higher your premium, the more coverage you usually get. Then, a deductible is the amount you have to shell out of your own pocket before your insurance kicks in to cover the rest. On certain healthcare services, you may also need to pay coinsurance, which is typically calculated as a percentage. If your coinsurance is 20%, you'll pay 20% of the covered service's cost, while your insurance covers the remaining 80%. It's like splitting the bill with your insurance company. Then, most plans also have out-of-pocket maximums where once you hit the maximum amount you'll have to pay, your insurance will cover all costs. So, when comparing plans, pay close attention to the terms and conditions of these costs. There are questionnaires you can take on many Insurance websites; just by answering a few questions regarding your healthcare, you will be given suggestions on what coverage is right for you.

Once you've decided which plan to choose, having it is not only about using it when you're sick—it's also about taking advantage of the preventive care services included in your plan, which may include annual check-ups, vaccinations, and screenings. So, take time to understand what's covered and what's not in your plan to save yourself from surprises when you least expect them. If you have a plan that's strict within its healthcare provider network, staying within the network can save you a bundle of costs. Plus, it's usually easier to manage claims and paperwork when you stay in the network.

Indeed, having health insurance feels like having a superhero cape for your health, but it doesn't guarantee that all your claims will always be approved. But don't worry. If your claims get denied, take a deep breath and review the denial letter carefully, as it should explain why the claim was denied and what steps you can take to appeal the decision. Don't hesitate to gather any necessary documentation or seek assistance from your healthcare provider. Or, when billing errors happen, reach out to the billing department or your insurance company to get it sorted out. Remember always to keep detailed records and documentation regarding your healthcare services.

EIGHT

Home Management Skills

Living on your own for the first time? Well, hang on because it's about to be a thrilling adventure. Getting used to this new phase of life can be like riding a bike without training wheels for the first time—you might wobble and find a few bumps, but ultimately, it's rewarding and way cooler than having someone constantly tell you what to do. That means you're in charge of everything, from making sure your fridge isn't packed with mold to finding the best deals while grocery shopping and fixing that leaky faucet that sounds like a rogue sprinkler. But hey, don't sweat it! Use it as a chance to unlock your hidden skills. You might surprise yourself by whipping up a healthy meal on a budget and mastering your laundry like your mom used to do. Plus, there's no one to judge your questionable cleaning techniques, so you can learn one step at a time without anyone's judgment.

Cooking 101: Eating Well on a Budget

Living on your own brings the dream of freedom to life, but it also means facing the reality that no one will be there to prepare your meals three times a day like your mom used to. Adulting often throws us into the kitchen with little to no cooking experience. However, with a few basic skills, you'll soon be whipping up dishes that are at least edible and, who knows, maybe even following recipes like a pro chef.

Let's start with the most fundamental cooking method: boiling. It is true when they say some people can't even boil water. It's perfect for softening vegetables like broccoli or potatoes, cooking pasta, and even poaching eggs for an easy breakfast. Just heat up a pot of water, add the ingredients, and let them simmer until they're cooked. You can save time by simply Googling how long each ingredient needs to cook. Simple, right? Next up is sautéing—all about adding quick bursts of flavor to your food. Just heat up a pan with some oil, throw in some onions and garlic, add your veggies or meat of choice, season with salt and pepper, and stir-fry until they're cooked through.

Now, let's move on to a slightly more complex method: baking. It's perfect for making fluffy cakes, cookies, and casseroles. Don't forget to preheat your oven to the specific temperature in your recipe before baking. Baking is ideal for busy schedules or when you want to impress your friends with minimal effort. Lastly, there's grilling, which adds that smoky, delicious flavor to your favorite meats or vegetables. Just preheat your grill, sear your food over high heat, and then lower the temperature to finish cooking it through.

Once you've mastered the basic cooking methods, recipes become your best friend. Ever stared at a recipe like it's written in a foreign language? Fear not! Reading and following recipes take time, but they are skills anyone can master. The ingredient list is basically your shopping list, so pay attention to quantities and units. Wash, chop, and measure all ingredients before you start cooking to avoid scrambling mid-recipe. During cooking, you may realize you forgot to buy a particular ingredient, spice, or herb. Don't worry! Just adapt based on what's available in your pantry. Who knows, it may turn out even tastier than the original recipe.

Cooking your own meals and having the freedom to eat whatever you like can easily lead to an unhealthy food spree. But remember your mom's advice—always eat your greens. Make sure you eat healthily, even on a tight budget. Eating healthy doesn't have to be expensive as long as you dedicate time each week to meal planning, avoiding unhealthy impulse buys, and ensuring you always have healthy ingredients. Explore your local farmers' market for fresh seasonal produce at great prices, especially when they're in season. Stock your pantry with healthy staples like beans, lentils, and whole wheat pasta for budget-friendly options. When you have leftovers, enjoy them for breakfast or lunch the next day, or transform them into a stir-fry, fried rice, or omelets. Most importantly, cook only what you'll eat to avoid food waste.

Grocery Shopping and Food Safety

Grocery shopping without your mom or dad beside you can be overwhelming, especially when you're trying to stick to a budget and make healthy choices. So, start by making a grocery list based on your meal plan for the week. Don't forget to check your pantry and kitchen to see what you already have. At the store, always look for sales and discounts on staple items, and don't forget to compare prices like your mom always did. Sometimes, the generic brand is just as good as the name brand but costs less. Plus, avoid strolling through processed foods, sugary drinks, and unhealthy snacks until the end of the shopping when you've already checked your grocery list. Also, never grocery shop while hungry, as it only leads to impulse purchases you might regret later.

When picking produce, look closely at fruits and vegetables, as they should be firm, brightly colored, and blemish-free. Choose lean cuts of meat with good marbling and a fresh smell. When buying packaged foods or drinks, make sure you understand food labels. First, pay attention to how many servings are in the package, as the nutrient details are based on that amount. Then, focus on nutrients like vitamins, minerals, fiber, and protein. Look for low amounts of saturated fat, sodium, and added sugars to keep your diet balanced. As ingredients are listed in descending order by weight, beware of sugar or unhealthy fats listed near the top. Watch out for common marketing tricks like low-fat claims or "all-natural," which can be misleading; focus only on the actual nutritional value.

When buying groceries, be sure to incorporate variety into your diet. To add variety to your meals, explore different fruits, vegetables, whole grains, legumes, nuts, seeds, and lean proteins. Healthy meals don't always have to be boring, so incorporate different textures and flavors to make meals more enjoyable. When you're done with groceries, proper food storage and handling ensure your food is safe from contamination and spoilage. Always store perishable foods, such as meat, poultry, seafood, dairy, and eggs, in the refrigerator or freezer to maintain freshness and prevent bacterial growth. Be vigilant in recognizing signs of food spoilage, such as unusual odors, textures, colors, or mold growth.

Nutrition and Balanced Eating

Taking care of ourselves means fulfilling all our macronutrient and micronutrient needs. Think of macronutrients as the lead actors in the production of your body, while micronutrients play the supporting cast. Your body needs macronutrients in large amounts to maintain optimal bodily functions, which come from carbohydrates, proteins, and fats. Carbohydrates are fast-acting energy boosters for your body, found in bread, pasta, rice, and fruits. Then, proteins help build and repair muscles, tissues, and organs and are contained in foods like meat, poultry, fish, beans, eggs, cheese, and yogurt. Despite fat often receiving a bad rap, it's essential for brain function, satiety, and absorbing vitamins, and is found in healthy sources like avocados, seeds, nuts, and olive oil.

Meanwhile, though needed in smaller amounts, micronutrients, which come from vitamins and minerals, play essential roles in keeping our bodies functioning at their best. Vitamins, sourced from fruits, vegetables, and supplements, help your body heal wounds, boost the immune system, and maintain sharp eyesight. Minerals keep your bones strong, your heart pumping, and your brain firing on all cylinders. They are sourced from dairy products, nuts, and whole grains. Ensuring you get a balanced diet means eating a variety of foods to fulfill your macronutrient and micronutrient needs.

But what if you're a vegan, skipping meat and dairy? Don't worry; plenty of plant-based goodies are packed with protein, fiber, vitamins, and minerals to keep you satisfied, like beans, lentils, tofu, nuts, seeds, and a rainbow of fruits and veggies. Or what if you have allergies to nuts, dairy, eggs, or gluten? Swap out allergens for safe alternatives, like almond milk instead of cow's milk or chickpea flour instead of wheat flour. Just be sure to read labels carefully to avoid any unwanted surprises. No matter your dietary needs or preferences, the key to maintaining a balanced diet is mixing and matching different foods to ensure you get all the nutrients your body needs to thrive.

Trying to be healthy and fulfill your daily nutrients also means minimizing sugar, processed foods, and excessive caffeine. These might seem harmless at first glance, but they can wreak havoc on our bodies if we're not careful. Instead of reaching for a candy bar or sugary drink that leads to weight gain or diabetes, opt for natural sources of sweetness like fruit and drizzles of honey. While processed foods might be convenient, they often lack nutrition due to their multiple processes and are packed with all sorts of additives and preservatives. So try to stick to whole, unprocessed food as much as possible. And let's not forget that too much caffeine can leave you feeling jittery and anxious and even mess with your sleep. So, try to limit your caffeine intake and choose water infused with fruits or herbal tea. The next time you find yourself craving chocolate cake or salty chips, ask yourself if it's truly hunger or just your body's way of signaling for something.

Keeping It Clean: Efficient Housekeeping Tips

Now that you're living on your own, taking care of your place is a big responsibility, but it can also be fun! To make it less overwhelming, divide household chores into daily tasks like making your bed, washing dishes, and emptying trash cans. Weekly chores include vacuuming floors, dusting furniture, and cleaning sinks, while monthly tasks involve cleaning out the refrigerator, washing bedding, or cleaning windows. Set a timer for short bursts of cleaning, each for 15-30 minutes, and you'll be surprised how much you can accomplish in your cleaning sprint.

When cleaning, avoid harsh chemicals that may not be good for your furniture or body. Whip up simple recipes using vinegar, baking soda, or lemon juice. These natural alternatives are effective at removing dirt and grime while being gentle on the environment and safe for daily use. Plus, they'll leave your home smelling fresh and clean without any synthetic fragrances.

While cleaning and decluttering, don't forget about regular home maintenance to save you big bucks down the road. Schedule tasks like changing air filters, cleaning gutters, and inspecting appliances to prevent costly repairs and extend their lifespan. Keep an eye out for signs of potential issues, like leaky faucets or clogged drains, and address them promptly. Plus, remember to wipe down appliance exteriors regularly to avoid dust buildup, which can lead to overheating and malfunction. Taking care of your place is an investment in your own well-being, so bring in a little effort, and you'll create a home that feels calm, functional, and clutter-free.

Basic Home Repairs: A DIY Guide for the Uninitiated

Living on your own is awesome, but unexpected things can break when you least expect them. That's why it's important to know how to do basic repairs to save some money.

- Have a leaky tap? First, shut off the faucet's water supply. Then, remove the handle and valve stem to access the inner components. Replace any worn-out washers, reassemble the faucet, and turn the water supply back on to check for leaks.
- Got a hole in the wall? Clean the area around the hole from any loose debris, apply patching compound, and smooth it. Let it dry completely before sanding down the patch until it's flush with the wall. Once dry, prime and paint the patched area to match the wall.

- Dealing with a clogged drain? Pour boiling water down the drains, followed by baking soda and vinegar to break down clogs. After letting it sit for half an hour, flush with hot water. Next time, make sure to remove hair or other debris from the drain every week or so.
- Lights out? Check the breaker box. If there's a tripped breaker, there may be an overload on the circuit. To reset it, switch the breaker to the off position, then back to the on position. If it trips again immediately, unplug devices from the affected circuit and try again. If the breaker continues to trip, there may be a larger electrical issue requiring professional assistance.

For these basic home repairs, make sure you own a screwdriver set, pliers, adjustable wrench, hammer, tape measure, flashlight, safety goggles, gloves, and putty knife.

To further prevent home damage, make sure you have a seasonal checklist to stick with. In the spring, check and replace air filters in your HVAC system and clean gutters to prevent water damage. In the summer, inspect hoses and sprinklers for leaks and test your smoke and carbon monoxide detectors. In the fall, clean leaves from gutters and downspouts and winterize outdoor faucets to prevent freezing. In the winter, check for drafts around windows and doors and seal them if necessary. Remember to insulate pipes to prevent freezing.

When you do home repairs and maintenance, always wear appropriate protective gear like goggles, gloves, and masks.

Then, follow manufacturer instructions and safety guidelines for tools and materials. Before starting a repair, remember to turn off electricity before electrical work or water when working on faucets or pipes. If unsure, you can always find out how to do simple home repairs on YouTube. If in doubt, know that you may need to call a professional for major electrical issues, major plumbing leaks, structural repairs, or anything you're not confident doing yourself.

Laundry Essentials: From Cleaning, Sorting, and Folding to Basic Repairs

Laundry is not exactly the most glamorous chore when you start living on your own, but it's essential for keeping your clothes clean and fresh whenever you need to wear them. Taking care of your laundry starts with separating your clothes based on colors and whether they are delicate or heavy. So, wash whites with whites, darks with darks, and colors together, but be cautious with new, brightly colored items that might bleed. Then, separate your clothes with thin and soft materials like silk, as they may need special care. Also, make sure towels, jeans, and other heavy fabrics go together. Whenever unsure, check clothing labels for specific instructions, such as washing temperatures and whether items should be washed separately.

When it comes to laundry products, select the best products for your needs based on fabric type, skin sensitivities, and whether there are stains. Powder detergents are great for tough stains and greasy clothes, while liquids are often gentler and better for cold water washes. You can also use pod detergents to make measuring easier and more convenient, but they come with pricier tags. For stained clothes, use stain removers before washing for better results.

When washing your clothes, avoid overloading the washer as it wrinkles clothes and reduces cleaning effectiveness. Plus, don't use too much detergent, as it can leave residue on clothes and lead to fabric damage. After washing, consider air-drying your clothes whenever possible, especially for delicate items, as it's gentler on clothes, prevents fading, and saves energy.

If you find minor damage on your clothes, don't toss them out right away—learn basic mending skills instead. If you've lost a button, thread a needle with a piece of thread that matches the garment, tie a knot at the end, insert the needle through one of the buttonholes, pull the needle through, and then insert it back through the opposite buttonhole. Repeat this process several times until you've created a tight stitch pattern. Once secure, finish by tying off the thread on the back of the fabric and trimming any excess. If you have a small rip on the seam of your clothes, turn the garment inside out, align the edges of the fabric, pin them together, insert a needle with matching thread through both layers of fabric, and pull it through. Continue stitching along the seam using a straight stitch. When you reach the end of the seam, tie off the thread securely. With practice, you'll become a pro at keeping your clothes looking their best for years to come.

Organizing Your Space: Tips for a Clutter-Free Life

Indeed, keeping a tidy home is like a never-ending game—it takes time, effort, and a whole lot of commitment. Sometimes, it feels easier to let those dishes stack up, the laundry pile on the floor, or miscellaneous items clutter the dining table. But what if I told you that maintaining a tidy space could significantly improve your overall quality of life? Imagine relaxing in a neat and tidy environment, feeling the stress melt away. Ahh, bliss! On the flip side, a cluttered mess can turn your brain into a tangled mess, making it difficult to concentrate, leading to reduced productivity and accuracy in your work (Mateo et al., 2013).

When your things feel cluttered, it's time to sort through them, keeping only what you need and love. Channel your inner Marie Kondo and ask yourself, "Does this spark joy?" If not, thank it for its service and let it go—whether to donate, sell, or recycle. If you haven't used it in a year, unless it's a sentimental item or something you use seasonally, it's probably time to say goodbye. Don't let the excuse "I might need it someday" stop you from decluttering; instead, give away anything you haven't used in a while.

Plus, invest in storage solutions like bins, baskets, and shelves to maximize space and efficiency. When considering new furniture, opt for pieces that serve multiple purposes, such as ottomans with storage compartments or futons that convert from a couch to a bed. Most importantly, make decluttering a regular habit by setting aside 10-15 minutes a day to keep things tidy. Always return items to their original spots after using them.

NINE

Communication and Relationships

Adulting involves immersing yourself in wider communities of family, friends, coworkers, and even romantic relationships. It's about expanding your social circle and building connections that enrich your life. That's where you need to develop your skills to navigate the intricate web of relationships that make up our lives through healthy, effective communication. It takes more than just being honest when sharing your views and emotions to make relationships last. It also takes listening well and having empathy for other people. Whenever conflicts arise, having effective communication means being open to finding solutions and compromises instead of resorting to insults and blame. So, learn these communication skills as you navigate adult life's complexities and watch your connections flourish and grow stronger over time.

The Basics of Effective Communication: Listening and Speaking

As you get older, no one will advocate for your needs, especially when you start living on your own. You need to get your ideas across effectively with coworkers, be a good friend, navigate dating life, and even communicate with your own parents. Effective communication is a two-way street; it's not just about getting your message across but also understanding what others say. That starts with being an active listener when communicating with anyone.

Yeah, I get it; you've been listening your whole life, right? But it's more than just hearing words and waiting for your turn to talk. It's about really tuning in and understanding the message. Put your phone aside, look people in the eye, and pay attention to them. Not only their words but also pay closer attention to body language and tone of voice, which can reveal much about their feelings. Most importantly, let them finish their thoughts before jumping in with your ideas. Then, show interest in what's being said by nodding occasionally, smiling at the person, and ensuring your posture is open and inviting. Whether in a team meeting, consulting with your boss, or chatting with friends and a significant other, being an active listener makes those communicating with you feel heard and understood, fostering stronger, deeper connections between you and them.

Being an active listener opens the door to effective communication. The next step you need to take is learning how to express yourself clearly while being respectful. It all starts with knowing your why. Before you speak, take a moment to clarify what you want to achieve in this communication—whether it's sharing ideas, resolving conflicts, or simply connecting with others. Then, opt for clear, concise language that accurately reflects your thoughts and feelings. Even during difficult conversations where emotions can run high, keep your feelings in check and maintain a calm demeanor to stay focused on the issue and avoid escalating the situation. Instead of assigning blame or passing judgment, focus more on how you can express your feelings and needs. Consider using "I" statements, such as replacing "You always make me stressed" with "I feel frustrated when this happens." Rather than solely aiming to make your point heard, strive to understand the other person's perspective as well. Put yourself in their shoes and consider how they might perceive your words.

Maintaining effective communication in relationships requires navigating potential barriers that may arise. As you enter adulthood and engage with wider communities, cultural differences become more and more apparent. So, respect and understand these barriers in communication styles and norms. Avoid making assumptions based on appearance or background, and approach conversations with an open mind. What you consider acceptable may not align with someone else's cultural norms. When communicating, also understand that emotions like anger or stress can sometimes hinder communication. Take time to cool down before expressing yourself or engaging with others to ensure clarity. Plus, when communicating, misinterpretation may happen all the time. So, always be specific and use examples or visuals to clarify complex concepts. Being mindful of these barriers can foster more effective communication and build stronger relationships.

Setting Boundaries: The Key to Healthy Relationships

Have you noticed that within your circle of friends, some enjoy hugs while others may not feel comfortable with that level of physical affection? Well, that's what's called boundaries. Sometimes, it's easy to assume that those who are okay with hugs are closer friends than those who aren't. But in reality, it's simply a matter of personal comfort and what each individual finds acceptable. Respecting these boundaries shows how sensitive and considerate you are to each person's preferences, fostering deeper understanding and respect not only within friendships but also in work settings. By honoring each other's boundaries, you can create a safe and comfortable environment where everyone feels valued and respected.

When it comes to setting boundaries, most people might not openly discuss what they find unacceptable unless they're very close to you. So, it's better to start respecting their boundaries by paying close attention to their verbal and nonverbal cues when interacting with them. If they seem uncomfortable, back away physically, or avoid eye contact, they might be setting a boundary. Notice what may be causing their discomfort, whether it's the conversation topic, a gesture, or anything else, and subtly adjust to give them some space. For example, if your coworker declines to hang out after work because they prefer to do things alone, don't pressure them to join. Instead, respect their "no" without trying to convince them otherwise or making them feel guilty for declining and assure them it's perfectly fine to opt out. Whenever you're unsure about someone's boundaries, open communication is the best approach. So, ask politely if a particular behavior is okay.

Aside from respecting others' boundaries and ensuring they feel respected, you also need to be aware of your own boundaries to protect your personal space, prevent inappropriate touching, and maintain privacy. Setting boundaries with people may be slightly uncomfortable for both you and others, so take it one step at a time. Remember that you are in control of your life, so take time to reflect and acknowledge what you cannot tolerate from others. Consider what makes you feel respected, safe, and comfortable, as well as situations or behaviors that make you feel uncomfortable. If you're still unsure about your own boundaries, pay attention to situations, behaviors, or interactions that often trigger discomfort and negative emotions within yourself, indicating where your boundaries lie. Once you've identified your personal limits, be assertive and direct yet respectful and non-confrontational when expressing your needs and preferences clearly to others. Consider using "I" statements, such as replacing "You make me uncomfortable" with "I feel uncomfortable when you do that." Be firm in asserting your limits, even if others may push back or try to guilt-trip you.

Even with the best communication, there will be times when someone oversteps your boundaries. So, instead of getting flustered, take a deep breath and gather your thoughts before responding. Use assertive communication to remind the person of your boundary, for example, saying, "I told you that I'm not comfortable discussing this." If the behavior continues, be more direct and consider communicating the consequences; don't tolerate them for the sake of avoiding conflict. For example, if a boundary violation occurs in a work setting, you could say, "If this issue persists, I may need to bring it to our supervisor for further resolution." Or, if it happens with friends or family, consider slowly creating space to limit interactions. Ultimately, when anyone consistently refuses to respect your boundaries, it's probably time to walk away. Your mental, emotional, and physical health should always come first. Surround yourself only with supportive individuals who respect and validate your boundaries.

Navigating Romantic Relationships: Communication and Compromise

Ah, the thrilling, wild world of romantic relationships! It's like a roller coaster of emotions that is full of exciting rides and heart-pounding twists and turns. But it's not just about the butterflies and lovey-dovey moments, although everyone dreams of having them. It's also about consciously maintaining the flame of love with a mix of trust, respect, and open communication. You've got to put in the effort to fill it with these gems, but what about the payoff? A love that keeps getting stronger and more caring over time. Don't you want to transform the heart-pounding crush stage into a healthy, lasting relationship? So, it all starts with trust—the sturdy foundation that everything else rests upon. It means feeling safe, secure, and confident that your partner has your back. You can be yourself without fear of judgment, and you know they'll be there through thick and thin. Then, treat your partner how you want to be treated—with respect. Beyond good manners, it means valuing your partner's thoughts, feelings, and decisions, even when disagreeing. That's why open communication that goes both ways is the key to a healthy romance, allowing each partner to communicate their deepest fears and wildest dreams. These three pillars—trust, respect, and open communication—work together to create a safe and supportive space where love can truly flourish. They allow you to weather any storm life throws your way because you know you have a solid foundation to build on.

However, even the strongest relationships hit bumps every now and then. When you try to create a strong bond between two different individuals, disagreements are inevitable. However, how you handle them can make all the difference through compromise. Compromise is not about giving up entirely; it's about finding a solution that works for both you and your partner so that no one feels like they're constantly giving in or getting the short end of the stick. So, always try to compromise even when arguing about little things, like when you love action flicks, but your partner prefers rom-coms. Then, pick a genre you can enjoy occasionally or try a new one together to expand your horizons. Or what if you're a spender while your partner is a saver? The answer is to create a budget that allows for both saving goals and having fun spending money. Or, when you're an extrovert but your partner's an introvert, find a sweet spot that balances social outings and quiet nights to cater to both preferences. The ultimate key is listening to your partner's needs or preferences and being open to new solutions.

When compromising, know that sometimes it may transform into having conflicts, but avoid sweeping issues under the rug only to find resentment build up. Instead, choose an appropriate time and place when you and your partner can calm down to discuss the issue. Avoid blaming or harshly criticizing your partner; after all, you've loved each other deeply, right? And stay focused on the problem at hand, not past grievances. Take turns expressing feelings, and then acknowledge your partner's perspective, even if you disagree. If emotions run high during a conflict, it's okay to take a break and revisit the discussion later when both partners have had time to cool off. Remember, the goal of conflict resolution is not to "win" the argument. It's about working together to find a solution that strengthens your relationship.

A few months into a new romantic relationship, everything feels magical and effortless, but as time passes, you may notice the initial spark beginning to fade. But it doesn't necessarily mean that the love is dwindling; instead, it's a sign that your relationship is transitioning into a deeper, more mature stage. Instead of waiting for the spark to return on its own, keep those conversations flowing about your hopes, dreams, and even everyday life, fostering understanding and more intimacy. Then, set aside dedicated time for date nights to keep romance alive, whether it's a candlelit dinner at home, a fun outing, or a weekend getaway. Or, explore shared hobbies and interests that you both enjoy, whether cooking together, taking dance lessons, or embarking on outdoor adventures. Most importantly, show appreciation for your partner's efforts, strengths, and contributions to the relationship and express gratitude even for the little things.

The Importance of Networking: Cultivating Professional Relationships

Working isn't just about completing assigned tasks on time for your boss; it's also about building networks. Networking with coworkers and other professionals allows you to tap into their experience, facilitating future collaborations. As a newcomer to the workplace, navigating work can be daunting, but a solid network provides a support system offering guidance, support, and advice. Beyond immediate benefits, investing time and effort to build a network fosters personal and professional growth, potentially opening doors to new opportunities and gaining valuable recommendations for future endeavors.

It all starts with getting to know not only your direct team but also colleagues across the team. Attend company events and engage in conversations. Not only within your current workplace, look for conferences, workshops, or online forums related to your field, which can be a great way to meet like-minded professionals. Also, follow companies and people you find interesting on LinkedIn, Instagram, or any other social media platforms, and don't be afraid to share relevant articles and participate in discussions to showcase your expertise as well.

While building a network is essential, maintaining it is equally important. Despite busy schedules, dedicate 10-15 minutes weekly to stay in touch with contacts. Instead of generic "hi there" messages, personalize your outreach by referencing specific aspects of their work or recent interactions. Share interesting articles or celebrate their achievements through messages or public shoutouts to show you care about their success. And when you see someone struggling, offer your expertise or refer them to relevant resources. If you're unsure how to find the just-right frequency to connect with your contacts, decide on weekly check-ins for close colleagues, while quarterly updates for wider connections might be appropriate. Remember, nurturing your network requires consistent effort, but the rewards in terms of professional development and opportunities are invaluable.

Dealing With Conflict: Strategies for Resolution

As you begin navigating a world filled with more complex relationships with friends, family, and romantic partners, conflicts are bound to arise. Whether it's disagreements with coworkers, misunderstandings with friends, differences of opinion with family members, or arguments with your significant other, learning how to navigate these conflicts is necessary instead of fearing them. Understand that clashes and drama mainly stem from miscommunication, where messages get garbled or misinterpreted, leading to frustration and tension. Differing values and beliefs can also ignite conflict, as individuals may have contrasting perspectives on various topics such as ethics, priorities, or goals, turning seemingly harmless topics into potential clashes even within our own families or close friendships. In a work setting, competition, whether for a promotion or a weekend activity, can also spark disagreements that might impact work performance. Understanding these common sources of conflict allows you to anticipate and recognize potential conflicts before they escalate and even prevent conflicts from arising altogether.

To prevent conflicts from catching you off guard, start by setting clear expectations, mainly, but not limited to, at work, right from the get-go to help avoid confusion and bitterness. Ensure that everyone knows their roles, responsibilities, and boundaries upfront. That way, there's less room for misunderstandings to escalate into full-blown showdowns. Then, when you find yourself on the brink of potential conflicts waiting to erupt, practice empathy by stepping into others' shoes and trying to understand where they're coming from. Most importantly, always foster a culture of open communication by encouraging everyone to speak up, share their thoughts, and address concerns directly. Conflicts are less likely to rear their heads when everyone feels heard and valued.

So, what happens when conflict erupts like a volcano, and how do you address it? With minor issues that aren't worth the fuss, the **avoidance** conflict management style might be appropriate, aiming to reduce conflict by ignoring it. Even though this style may seem like sweeping issues under the rug, it can give people much-needed time to calm down, gather their thoughts, and rethink their perspectives. Or, with issues where you want to keep the peace and maintain harmony, using the **accommodation** style may be a great idea, simply putting other parties' needs before your own. It's a way of allowing them to "win" and move on. While it might seem like you make yourself "lose," the accommodation style can be the best choice when facing a minor conflict where you just want to move on to more important issues. Lastly, the **collaboration** style is probably the best long-term result, yet the most challenging and time-consuming to achieve. With the collaboration style, your and the other parties' needs and wants are considered so everyone leaves satisfied. It starts with all parties sitting down together, with a third person or not, to talk through the actual conflict and create a solution together. Know that this style may take a long time, depending on the parties involved and the issue itself.

TEN

Practical Life Skills

A dulting is not merely about finally having no one to restrict your bedtime, tell you not to eat ice cream for breakfast, or forbid ordering pizza in the middle of the night. The real challenge lies in the everyday. It is about navigating the decision maze of whether to purchase a car, deciphering public transportation schedules, and the constant battle between packing light and bringing everything "just in case" for a trip. So, here is a chapter to help you embrace the chaos, relish the challenges, and find delight in the small wins along the way.

Transportation and Travel

Have you decided to purchase a new or used car? It is impossible to determine which choice is preferable for every situation. It is a very personal decision that you cannot take lightly since it will eventually affect your finances. Is purchasing a new car more expensive than a used car?

Indeed, a new car is much more costly than buying a used car, but it does not necessarily mean buying a used car is more affordable. Even though the initial expenses for purchasing a used car can be much cheaper, having a used car can sometimes be more expensive than a new one if it has many defects from the previous owner. And that's the biggest downside of purchasing a used car, which is that you might not know some defects exist, especially if you're not a car enthusiast. In contrast, since new cars are delivered in the best possible condition, flaws are usually not an issue when purchasing a new car. However, when purchasing a new car, consider its great depreciation, as you almost throw away up to 10% of the car's value the minute you drive off the lot (Hawley, 2024). Either choice is great when taking into account all the requirements for both new and used cars, as long as you carefully evaluate your unique circumstances. Besides, because it will have a substantial long-term financial impact, you should take into account both the initial cost and recurrent expenses.

To ensure you get the best value possible when purchasing a new car, always research the market value of the vehicle you're interested in buying. Compare it with similar models, makes, and years to get a clear picture of what the vehicle is worth. Similarly, to improve your negotiating position when purchasing a used car, create a price range based on the vehicle's book value, which is determined by subtracting the car's cumulative depreciation from its original cost. Consider buying when dealerships offer promotions or incentives, such as end-of-year clearance sales or holiday sales events. Additionally, wait until the buying environment cools down, especially during high inflation. You'll probably find more reasonably priced cars and better credit rates in a more relaxed market. When comparing financing options, look around for appealing offers and great deals on rates that set one financing option apart. New vehicles often have lower interest rates on loans compared to used vehicles. Above all, when choosing financing options, be realistic about the kind of car you really need, how much you can afford, and how much of a monthly payment you can manage.

As you now have your own car, applying for car insurance is the next thing you must do to better prepare yourself against hefty financial losses and bills due to accidents, theft, vandalism, and other unforeseen events. Besides, it's also mandatory by law in certain states. Despite how careful you are on the road, accidents can strike at any time and anywhere. Not sure how to start? Begin by scouring insurance providers through referrals from your friends and family who already have car insurance and can share their personal experiences. Then, choose the type of coverage that matches your needs, whether liability, collision, or comprehensive coverage. Keep in mind that insurance costs may depend on your driving record, car type, location, and annual mileage, so shop around with different providers to get the best rate. Anytime you have a car loan, you must have full coverage for Insurance. In addition to car insurance, it's wise to consider applying for gap insurance. This coverage fills the gap between your vehicle's actual cash value and the amount you still owe on your loan if your car is totaled or stolen. However, gap insurance may not be suitable for everyone unless you have a low down payment, finance a new car (which depreciates quickly), or have a long loan term. So, consider whether gap insurance is necessary based on these factors.

Similarly, when it comes to selling your car, whether it's because your vehicle no longer fits your needs or you're moving to a more walkable area where a car isn't necessary, understanding your car's current market value is crucial in deciding if it's a buyer's market or if you should hold onto it a while longer. While not always absolute, some trends do exist; for example, trucks tend to sell better in the spring and summer, while convertibles do well closer to summer. Next, ensure your car is well-maintained with a documented service history, which can boost the price and help it sell faster. Consider a professional detail and address any minor repairs that might deter buyers. You tend to receive more money for your vehicle if sold outright compared to trading it in at a dealership.

Whether you want to maintain resale value or ensure longevity in using the car, giving your vehicle regular essential car maintenance is vital. Not only does it keep your car looking shiny, but maintaining the condition of brakes, tires, and lights plays a crucial role in safe driving. Here are basic car maintenance tasks you should check off as a car owner:

- **Oil and filter:** As they are the lifeblood of your engine, make sure you clean and replace them regularly, typically every 5,000-7,500 miles (if using regular oil) and 7,500-10,000 miles (if using synthetic oil) to reduce friction. Always check your manual to see what is best for your vehicle.

- **Tires:** Remember to rotate your tires to ensure even wear and tear and maximize their lifespan. Tires should be inspected regularly for proper inflation, tread depth, and signs of damage.
- **Brakes:** As they are paramount for safety, regularly check the pads for wear and tear and have a mechanic inspect the entire braking system periodically. Signs of brake problems include squealing or grinding noises, pulsating brakes, or a soft brake pedal.
- **Fluids:** Check fluid levels, including engine oil, coolant, transmission fluid, brake fluid, and power steering fluid, as low fluid levels may indicate leaks or other issues.
- **Lights:** Ask someone to take a quick walk around the vehicle to ensure the headlights, taillights, brake lights, and turn signals function properly.

Most importantly, to maintain your car's condition, find a reliable mechanic. Get recommendations from friends and family or scour online reviews. Also, look for mechanics with certifications like ASE (Automotive Service Excellence). Then, keep detailed records of all maintenance and repairs performed on your vehicle, including dates, mileage, and invoices to help track the car's maintenance history. This may also be useful for warranty claims or resale purposes.

Even with regular maintenance, car emergencies can still occur every now and then. So, having a solid emergency plan is the ultimate key to handling most common emergencies safely and getting back on the road quickly. Have a flat tire? Immediately pull over to a safe location away from traffic, and remember to turn on your hazard lights. If you have a spare tire and know how to change it, carefully jack up your car and make the switch. But if you're unsure or don't have the necessary tools, call roadside assistance or wait for help from a professional. Did your car battery die? If you have jumper cables and another vehicle with a working battery, you can attempt a jump-start by following the proper procedure, ensuring both cars are turned off and the cables are connected correctly. If jump-starting doesn't work or you don't have access to jumper cables, call roadside assistance or a towing service. Notice your car overheating? Pull over to a safe location and turn off the engine immediately to prevent further damage. Allow the engine to cool down before opening the radiator cap or checking the coolant level for at least 30 minutes to an hour. If the coolant is low, add more coolant or water if coolant isn't available. But if you notice any leaks, call for roadside assistance. To better prepare yourself when facing emergencies, ensure you have an emergency car kit in place with essential tools like a spare tire, portable tire inflator, jack, jumper cables, flashlight, first aid kit, reflective triangles, and water or snacks to keep you energized during emergencies.

Public Transportation Tips

For many of you, not having a car means you must deal with constant scrambling and complicated commutes. Sure, navigating unfamiliar schedules and maps can feel overwhelming at first. But once you get the hang of it, public transportation can be a breeze! Not only is it a budget-friendly way to get around, but it's also your way of contributing to reducing air pollution, carbon emissions, and traffic congestion.

To make navigating public transportation more manageable, take some time before starting your day to familiarize yourself with the routes, schedules, and maps of the public transportation system in your city. Learn about the different types of public transportation available: buses, trains, trams, or subways, so you can choose the best line to reach your destination effectively. In most areas, you can find details online or through mobile apps, which can suggest the most efficient routes based on your starting point. Be aware of fare options offered, such as single rides, day passes, or monthly passes. Aim to arrive at stations or stops a few minutes early to avoid rushing during peak hours. Most importantly, stay updated on any service changes, delays, or disruptions that may affect your travel plans. If you're still unsure of the schedules and routes, don't be afraid to ask for directions or help from staff or fellow passengers. Most people are happy to guide you.

Public transportation is a shared space, so be mindful of others' comfort to make the experience enjoyable for everyone. It starts with always being respectful of others' personal space. Avoid crowding others, and don't spread out with your belongings. Keep noise levels down by avoiding loud phone conversations or playing music on speakers. As a young and healthy person, consider giving up your seat to passengers who need it more, like the elderly, pregnant women, or people with disabilities, if no other seats are available. Be considerate of others by avoiding strong perfumes, eating messy food, or bringing large packages that block the aisle.

Learning about public transportation maps and routes isn't the hardest part of using them. However, there's a slightly increased risk of getting pickpocketed or harassed. Whenever you're using public transportation, keep your valuables close to your body and avoid using headphones at high volumes so you can stay alert to your surroundings, especially during crowded times. If you find yourself in an unsafe situation, trust your instincts and move to a well-lit area, inform a staff member, or disembark at the next stop if necessary. If you ever need to commute at night, plan your arrival at a well-lit stop close to your final destination. If you're unfamiliar with the area, consider using another form of public transportation, like a taxi or ride-sharing service, for the last leg of your journey.

Planning and Packing for Travel

Mastering practical skills goes beyond just navigating your daily routine and deciding on your mode of commute, whether it's your own car or public transportation. It's also about embracing a fair share of thrills, spills, and wanderlust-filled chills when traveling around your familiar places, whether it's for a career conference, pursuing higher education across the globe, or that long-awaited solo adventure. If you were used to waiting for your mom to pack up for a road trip, now's the time to start learning about planning and packing for travel on your own.

It all begins with knowing where you're headed. Browse travel blogs, explore online forums, or even consult guidebooks to envision your travel experience, considering factors like location, weather, and tourism destinations. Once you have a vision of your trip, start exploring accommodations before booking. Whether you're a luxury seeker or a budget-conscious traveler, there's always a perfect place to rest your weary head. Consider location, amenities, and guest reviews when choosing, and don't forget to explore online booking platforms to compare prices and snag the best deals available.

If you're planning to travel abroad, start preparing for your passport application procedures, which typically involve submitting proof of citizenship, a government-issued photo ID, and other relevant documents. Depending on whether you're applying for a new passport or renewing an existing one and how quickly you need it, application fees may vary. Be prepared to pay the required fee and allow ample time for processing, as it can take several weeks to receive your passport. As soon as you receive your passport, double-check the details for accuracy.

Most importantly, ensure you set a realistic budget for your trip, from booking accommodations and flight tickets to activities and passport application fees. Yet, remember that budgeting doesn't have to mean sacrificing the fun you're about to have. To ensure your budget is realistic, use travel websites, blogs, and forums to get a sense of average costs for your chosen destination. Plus, don't forget to factor in some wiggle room for unexpected expenses or spontaneous adventures.

Once you're all set with your passport, accommodations booking, and flight ticket, it's time to tackle the most loved and hated process before traveling for most: packing. It's not just about piling up all your wardrobe in your luggage; it's about packing your needs effectively as different types of travel call for different packing strategies. For shorter trips, pack versatile clothing pieces that can be mixed and matched to create multiple outfits. While for longer trips, prioritize lightweight and wrinkle-resistant items. Also, consider the purpose of your travel. To avoid forgetting any essentials or overpacking, consider making a list beforehand. Quite a few packing apps give suggestions on what to pack for specific climates.

While traveling doesn't mean you're immune to medical emergencies, invest in travel insurance to provide peace of mind and financial protection. Also, research whether you need vaccinations or health advisories for your destination. And don't forget to pack essentials like pain relievers, bandages, and antiseptic wipes.

Before setting foot in a new adventure waiting for you, take the time to familiarize yourself with the local customs, traditions, and social norms, whether it's dressing modestly, observing certain local etiquettes, avoiding insulting gestures, or respecting traditions, especially in sacred areas. Embrace moments of connection with locals, whether it's sharing a meal, participating in a traditional ceremony, or simply engaging in conversation.

While traveling is an adventure, always prioritize your safety from pickpockets or scams. Keep your belongings secure at all times, and make copies of important documents like your passport, ID, and travel insurance documents. Be wary of overly friendly strangers or unsolicited offers of assistance, and avoid visiting unfamiliar areas, especially at night. Research potential scams specific to your destination and stay informed about local safety concerns. Trust your gut; if something feels off, it probably is.

ELEVEN

Legal and Civic Responsibilities

Adulting is more than being free to do whatever you want or staying up late. It also comes with a whole new set of responsibilities that can indeed be complex at first. It's a landscape where understanding the law is not just a matter of avoiding trouble but a cornerstone of empowerment and accountability as a responsible citizen. Your voice is not merely representative of what will happen to you; it's also contributing to shaping the collective future of society. Well, it might seem overwhelming at first, but at the same time, it's empowering, right? It means you have a say in your life, your community, and the world around you. So, start by knowing your legal and civic responsibilities to make informed choices and contribute to a better future.

Understanding Your Legal Rights

Being a responsible citizen starts with knowing your legal rights to protect yourself and ensure you get fair treatment in everyday situations. First and foremost, you have privacy rights that protect you from unwarranted intrusion into your personal affairs, including unauthorized surveillance, searches, and seizures. You have the right to keep certain information confidential, such as medical records, financial information, and personal communications, unless law enforcement has a warrant to access your devices or online accounts. Especially in this digital age, you have the right to decide which information companies can collect and use. At work, your workplace must ensure a safe working environment and fair treatment against discrimination based on race, gender, age, or disability, including fair compensation for your work. Educate yourself about labor laws and employment rights specific to your field. When interacting with law enforcement officers, know your rights to protect yourself from potential abuses of power. You have the right to remain silent, to refuse consent to searches, and to request legal representation if you're arrested. If you want to learn more and find support for your legal rights, refer to the American Civil Liberties Union (ACLU) at www.aclu.org or The National Legal Aid & Defender Association (NLADA) at www.nlada.org. Also, consider searching for legal aid services around your community that can provide legal advice or representation at a low cost or even for free.

From renting an apartment, starting a new job, or borrowing money, most adult transactions come with the need to understand different contracts. A contract exists to legally bind the agreement between you and other parties, outlining rights, responsibilities, and obligations. So every time you need to sign one, always read the fine print by paying close attention to crucial details, especially payment terms, termination clauses, and any penalties for breach of contract. When you find conditions that don't fit your needs and preferences well, don't hesitate to negotiate them out as long as you are reasonable about the changes. If one party fails to fulfill their obligations under the contract, it constitutes a breach. So, if you find yourself in this situation, keep documents of all communications and evidence related to the breach. Seek legal advice so you can weigh your options and get advice on potential legal recourse depending on the breach's severity.

When you encounter disputes with landlords, unexpected contract breaches, or even traffic violations, know your rights to find the right-fit lawyer, especially in complex legal situations, as they specialize in different areas. Select one whose experience is relevant to your circumstances to defend your interests and help you navigate the legal system. After you've chosen a lawyer, an initial consultation is necessary so you can clarify your objectives, and they can provide you with a roadmap for moving forward. Then, educate yourself on the legal proceedings, which generally involve pleadings, discovery, pretrial motions, trial, and appeal. Understanding these steps in legal proceedings can help you prepare for what to expect.

Civic Engagement and Voting

Don't you dream of positively impacting your community or even your country? Voting is your way to stand up for the issues you care most about, like affordable housing, national security, environmental protection, crime, and immigration. So, when you choose not to vote, you're losing your voice to improve your community. Your vote, and every vote, is a needed contribution to shaping the trajectory of our society and advancing the common good. Start by registering to vote —it's the first step toward participating in the democratic process. Depending on your state's laws and regulations, you may be able to register online, by mail, or in person at designated registration sites. Or, access www.usa.gov/register-to-vote to download the national mail voter registration form, where you can fill out the form on-screen and print the completed form. Before mailing the form to the address provided for your state, don't forget to sign it. Beyond voting, make sure you understand the electoral process, including how elections are conducted, the roles of different elected officials, and the significance of various ballot measures and initiatives to recognize and challenge efforts to suppress voting rights.

Beyond voting, civic engagement is all about how you can participate in communities and work together to make things better, like volunteering, attending town hall meetings, and advocating. Volunteering, whether it's serving meals at a soup kitchen, tutoring students, cleaning up parks, or participating in community events, fosters a sense of belonging and strengthens social bonds within the community. Town hall meetings provide residents with the opportunity to voice concerns, ask questions, and engage directly with community leaders. No matter how you choose to participate, civic engagement is a great start to actually making a difference in your community rather than only complaining about it.

Navigating Government and Public Services

Other than acknowledging your responsibilities as a citizen, be aware that you also have the right to access government services. Firstly, the government provides healthcare services to ensure access to affordable and quality healthcare for all citizens. Depending on your country, these services may include public healthcare programs, insurance schemes, and subsidized medical services. Also, the government provides education services for its students, ranging from public schools to colleges, universities, and vocational training programs, aiming to provide accessible education. Moreover, the government offers a wide range of social programs and assistance to individuals and families in need, including welfare programs, housing assistance, unemployment benefits, and childcare support. To access these government and public services, be aware of their eligibility criteria and apply for benefit programs as needed. Dealing with the bureaucracy of implementing these services may be complicated, so start by familiarizing yourself with relevant laws, regulations, and procedures. Keep thorough documentation of your interactions with government agencies, including forms, correspondence, and receipts. Also, be patient and persistent in following up on your applications or requests, and don't hesitate to seek assistance if you encounter disputes.

Alongside ensuring you get your rights, remember your responsibilities as a citizen. The most fundamental responsibility is obeying the laws to ensure order, safety, and justice for all. By obeying laws, we contribute to the stability and well-being of our communities. Paying your taxes is a way to fund essential public services and infrastructure that benefit you. But remember, as a taxpayer, you have the right to advocate for transparency and accountability in tax policies and government spending to ensure that tax dollars are used efficiently. Also, fulfilling civic duty means you must report for jury duty whenever you receive a summons. When you receive this summons, it indicates that you have been randomly selected from a list of registered voters, licensed drivers, or other sources, depending on the jurisdiction, to ensure a fair and impartial jury. Thus, you are expected to fulfill your jury duty obligations unless you or a family member has a conflict of interest in the case being tried, which could compromise your ability to be impartial. Apart from that, failing to respond to a jury summons or to appear for jury duty without a lawful excuse can lead to legal consequences such as fines or even being held in contempt of court.

TWELVE

Community Engagement and Personal Growth

Now that you've become a real adult, not just dreaming about being one, life feels more significant than you and your needs. You start noticing the cracks in the sidewalk you trip on every day, the overflowing recycling bins down the street, or the community center that could use a fresh coat of paint. That is where your heart starts wanting to lend a hand where you can through community engagement. It is about realizing your actions can ripple outwards, making your corner of the world a little brighter. Not only does it benefit your community, but it also feeds right back into you with the good feeling of helping others, building connections, and exposing you to new experiences.

Through volunteering, you might learn or discover a passion. And guess what? This growth doesn't have an expiration date. As you age, you can keep seeking new ways to engage and learn, from taking an online course to being a mentor to a young entrepreneur to trying to live more sustainably.

Remember, adulthood is a lifelong adventure, and the destination is constantly evolving—just like you.

Volunteering: Giving Back and Growing

Volunteering isn't just about helping others; it helps you the most by allowing you to test-drive your talents or learn entirely new ones. Volunteering connects you with like-minded people who may someday become your future mentor, business partner, or lifelong friends with those who share your passion for making a difference. Plus, helping others gives you a sense of purpose amidst combating stress and depression on your journey to adulthood. To ignite these sparks within you, finding your perfect volunteer match is key. Ask yourself, what are you genuinely enthusiastic about? Is it volunteering at a shelter? Feeding the Homeless? Spending time at an animal shelter? Search for an organization that aligns with your interests for a more fulfilling experience. Or do you need a platform to showcase your skills? Make sure you are volunteering in an organization to leverage your existing skills. What kind of impact do you want to make—whether helping underprivileged youth, promoting environmental sustainability, or supporting veterans? Find one whose values resonate with yours the most. Think of volunteering as a chance to step outside your comfort zone, so be open to feedback and guidance from experienced volunteers and staff.

Even though volunteering brings out the best in you, it does not have to become another burden filling your entire plate.

Assess available time and commitments realistically and identify opportunities within those parameters. Do you only have a short spare time? Find organizations that need help with one-time tasks or virtual projects. Or, find ones that enable you to commit to volunteer roles with flexible scheduling options. To maintain balance and ensure that volunteering remains a rewarding experience, setting boundaries, communicating availability with volunteer coordinators, and practicing self-care are key.

Lifelong Learning: The Path to Personal and Professional Development

As the world is in a constant state of flux, the skills you have today might not be enough tomorrow. Make sure to prioritize lifelong learning to unlock your full potential and stay ahead of the curve. Learning new things keeps your mind sharp and opens doors to exciting hobbies, interests, and even careers you never knew existed. Remind yourself that the possibilities of learning are endless. Whether it is a new technology at work or a shift in social trends, continuous learning keeps you on your toes and ready to tackle whatever comes your way. So, choose your way of learning wisely— whether through taking online courses, attending workshops or events, experiential learning, or even the simplest method, through books. Find what excites you most about learning, whether online or in-person, solo or in a group. Even if you do not fancy connecting with others while learning, set aside some time for reading that stimulates your brain, broadens your perspectives, and keeps you learning even when you only have 10-15 minutes every day.

Now that you are pumped to learn, make it a sustainable habit by aiming for specific, measurable, attainable, relevant, and time-bound (SMART) goals. Keep a log of your learning journey, and track the courses you've completed or the new skills you have mastered. Also, surround yourself with people who share your passion for learning by joining online communities, attending meetups, or finding a buddy to learn. Aside from making the journey much more enjoyable, having a support system keeps you accountable. Once you gain your newfound knowledge, don't let it gather dust. Revamp your resume to reflect specific job descriptions, showcasing how your learning directly relates to the desired qualifications. Or, share your newfound expertise with colleagues at work or offer to lead a training session. Don't worry about facing resistance because your company would likely appreciate you taking the initiative to learn outside of what the company has provided.

The Power of Mentorship: Being a Mentor and Finding One

The whirlwind of adulthood, where responsibilities seem to pile up faster than we can keep track, can feel like navigating rough waters without a compass. That's precisely why having a mentor by your side can make all the difference, helping you chart your course and weather any storm. If you're unfamiliar with mentoring, it's essentially a dynamic connection where a more seasoned person, known as the mentor, offers advice, knowledge, and support to a less seasoned person, known as the mentee, to assist them in navigating their personal and professional growth. However, mentorship isn't a one-way street; both the mentor and the mentee gain from it. Mentors gain satisfaction from sharing their expertise, expanding their networks, and honing their communication skills. Meanwhile, mentees benefit from the mentor's experience, insights, and confidence in their abilities.

However, finding a mentor can be challenging, especially someone you can get along with. Start by seeking mentors within your current organization, professional associations, alumni networks, or through social media platforms. When reaching out to potential mentors, personalize your message to stand out and clearly articulate what you hope to gain from the relationship. Once you have a mentor, remember that the responsibility doesn't fall solely on them. You need to be proactive and work with your mentor to establish clear goals, showing your commitment to learning. Most importantly, stay in touch with your mentor between meetings to update them on your progress or ask follow-up questions.

To ensure your mentorship is a two-way street, remember to thank them for their time and guidance, as appreciation goes a long way. You can also offer support in return for a project or connect them with someone in your network. Someday, you might even want to become a mentor yourself. However, being a mentor is not easy; it requires empathy, patience, and a genuine desire to help others succeed. Mentors should strive to empower mentees, foster a growth mindset, and celebrate their successes.

Embracing Cultural Diversity: Learning From Others

As adulting exposes you to wider and more diverse communities, it calls for your openness to embrace diversity. After all, everyone has different ways of thinking, living, and experiencing the world. This diversity fosters creativity, innovation, and problem-solving, offering a whole new outlook by bringing together a variety of viewpoints and experiences. Further, cultural diversity promotes tolerance, empathy, and mutual respect, laying the foundation for harmonious community relations. It all starts with a willingness to learn and openness to new experiences, whether through books, documentaries, or cultural events. When engaging with individuals from diverse backgrounds, challenge yourself to have meaningful conversations, and do not hesitate to ask respectful questions to deepen understanding and challenge stereotypes. While curiosity is critical to learning more about them, remember to be sensitive and avoid making assumptions.

Though others' beliefs and values may differ greatly from yours, try to put yourself in their shoes and understand their experiences to foster cross-cultural relationships. Instead of seeing differences as barriers, celebrate them and value the unique contributions each person brings to the relationship. By getting close to those whose backgrounds differ from yours, you can contribute even more to a culture of inclusion. Speak up for fair representation and challenge discriminatory practices in your workplace or community. Actively support those facing discrimination and promote understanding and respect for all cultures. By embracing cultural diversity and fostering inclusion, we create a richer, more vibrant world for everyone. We can all play a role in building bridges across cultures, promoting understanding, and creating a world where everyone feels valued and respected.

Sustainability and You: Living an Eco-Friendly Life

When you've become older, you might just realize how impactful a healthy environment is for people's well-being and survival. Pollution and overuse of natural resources can lead to climate change, habitat loss, and resource depletion. Through sustainable living, we can protect our planet and avoid making choices that leave it in a mess for future generations. It doesn't have to be about making big changes all at once in your daily life, but you can start small by reducing waste, like saying no to single-use plastic and opting for reusable alternatives. Choose products with minimal packaging and support businesses with sustainable practices. Also, try conserving energy by switching off those lights, unplugging those unnecessary chargers, and maybe even investing in solar power. Furthermore, it's time to embrace green transportation by opting for walking, biking, taking public transport, or carpooling whenever possible to reduce your carbon footprint significantly.

It's easy to feel like these small actions are insignificant in making a difference, but the power lies in numbers. When millions of people make small changes towards sustainability, the collective impact is enormous. So, let's get your friends, family, and community on board with these sustainability changes. How? Start by leading by example. Show off your eco-friendly swaps and share your sustainability wins on social media. Spread the word about the benefits of sustainability—like how it saves money, protects nature, and makes you feel like a total planet-saving hero. Making sustainability fun and social is the best way to get everyone excited about saving the world together!

Conclusion

Remember that first chapter when you were just starting out on this journey to become the best version of yourself? You were filled with uncertainties and questions about navigating the complex world of adult life. But look at you now! You've come a long way from understanding basic financial principles and thriving in the ever-evolving digital world to making meaningful contributions to those around you. And guess what? This isn't the end of the road. You can still turn to this book whenever you need guidance on life's twists and turns.

Throughout your journey with this book, you've discovered the power of personal growth and resilience. You've learned to adapt, overcome obstacles, and bounce back from setbacks —all essential ingredients for a fulfilling and successful life. But remember, the learning never truly stops. Keep that hunger for knowledge alive! Embrace new experiences, stay curious, and continuously reflect on your progress. A growth mindset is your most valuable asset.

As you step into the real world, take a deep breath—tell yourself, you've got this! Challenges will come, and that's inevitable. But with the skills you've acquired, you're now better equipped to face them head-on. And hey, you're not alone in this journey. Everyone, at some point in their lives, has faced confusion in navigating the journey of adulthood. And when things start to feel overwhelming, never hesitate to ask for assistance, whether from friends, family, or even professionals. No journey is complete without a supportive community by your side. Remember the importance of building and relying on those around you for guidance and encouragement.

As you close this chapter and look towards the future, remember that learning is a lifelong journey. So, don't let these lessons gather dust on a shelf. Put them into action! Start small, integrate these strategies into your daily life, and witness the positive transformations unfold. This book, hopefully, has served as a valuable guide on your path to independence and success. And while challenges may arise every now and then, you now have the knowledge and skills to face them head-on. Welcome to Adulting!

References

Bethune, S. (2014, April). *Teen stress rivals that of adults.* American Psychological Association. https://www.apa.org/monitor/2014/04/teen-stress

Davis, D. M., & Hayes, J. A. (2012, July). *What are the benefits of mindfulness?* American Psychological Association. https://www.apa.org/monitor/2012/07-08/ce-corner

Federal Student Aid. (2022). *4 loan forgiveness programs for teachers.* Studentaid.gov. https://studentaid.gov/articles/teacher-loan-forgiveness-options/

Fennell, A. (2022, November). *How long recruiters spend looking at your CV | 2023 study.* StandOut CV. https://standout-cv.com/how-long-recruiters-spend-looking-at-cv#:

Hanson, M. (2022, May 25). *How many people have student loans (as of 2021)? | Analysis.* Education Data Initiative website: https://education-data.org/how-many-people-have-student-loans

Hawley, R. (2024, April 02). *Car depreciation: What it is and how it works.* Bankrate. https://www.bankrate.com/insurance/car/understanding-car-depreciation/

Mateo, R., Hernández, J. R., Jaca, C. & Blazsek, S. (2013). Effects of tidy/messy work environment on human accuracy. *Management Decision,* (51), 1861-1877. https://doi.org/10.1108/MD-02-2013-0084

Petrosyan, A. (2024, January 31). *Worldwide digital population 2024.* Statista. https://www.statista.com/statistics/617136/digital-population-worldwide/

Sharma, A., Madaan, V., & Petty, F. D. (2006). Exercise for mental health. *Primary Care Companion to the Journal of Clinical Psychiatry,* 8(2), 106. https://doi.org/10.4088/pcc.v08n0208a

Tolbert, J., Orgera, K., & Damico, A. (2022, December 19). *Key Facts about the uninsured population.* Kaiser Family Foundation. https://www.kff.org/uninsured/issue-brief/key-facts-about-the-uninsured-population/

Transamerica Center for Retirement Studies. (2022). *Emerging from the COVID-19 pandemic: A compendium about U.S. workers' retirement outlook.* Transamerica Center for Retirement Studies.

https://transamericainstitute.org/docs/default-
source/research/emerging-from-covid-19-pandemic-compendium-
worker-retirement-outlook-report.pdf

United States Census Bureau. (2022). *Health insurance coverage in the
United States: 2021*. In United States Census Bureau. https://www.-
census.gov/library/publications/2022/demo/p60-278.html

www.ingramcontent.com/pod-product-compliance
Lightning Source LLC
Chambersburg PA
CBHW030255130626
46549CB00002B/539